The Will of God

The Will of God

*Moral and Political Guidance
from Calvin's Commentaries on the Mosaic Law*

ALEX SOTO

RESOURCE *Publications* · Eugene, Oregon

THE WILL OF GOD
Moral and Political Guidance from Calvin's Commentaries on the Mosaic Law

Copyright © 2012 Alex Soto. All rights reserved. Except for brief quotations in critical publications or reviews, no part of this book may be reproduced in any manner without prior written permission from the publisher. Write: Permissions, Wipf and Stock Publishers, 199 W. 8th Ave., Suite 3, Eugene, OR 97401.

Resource Publications
An Imprint of Wipf and Stock Publishers
199 W. 8th Ave., Suite 3
Eugene, OR 97401
www.wipfandstock.com

ISBN 13: 978-1-61097-753-1

Manufactured in the U.S.A.

All scripture quotations, unless otherwise indicated, are taken from the New King James Version®. Copyright © 1982 by Thomas Nelson, Inc. Used by permission. All rights reserved.

To the memory of Bill Winter,
whose delight in the Law of his Lord always encouraged me

It is an inestimable benefit when God shows us His will.

—Calvin, Sermon on Deuteronomy 28:1–2

Contents

Acknowledgments ix
Introduction xi

Preface to the Decalogue / 1
First Commandment: *No False Gods* / 19
Second Commandment: *No Human Inventions in Worship* / 33
Third Commandment: *No Irreverent Talk of God* / 49
Fourth Commandment: *Meditate on God's Works* / 57
Fifth Commandment: *Obey Superiors* / 63
Sixth Commandment: *No Disrespecting Life* / 69
Seventh Commandment: *No Unchastity* / 81
Eighth Commandment: *No Unjust Gains* / 97
Ninth Commandment: *No Slander* / 121
Tenth Commandment: *No Coveting* / 125
Sum and Use of the Law / 127

Bibliography / 131
Scripture Indices
    A: Calvin's Expositional Order / 135
    B: Calvin's Decalogical Division in Canonical Order / 139
    C: Canonical Order / 143

Acknowledgments

My special thanks to those who helped make this book possible: Ann-Marie Hines, Ernie Monroe, Seth Nelson, Jim Pelletier, Peter Stazen, Jeff Van Every, and Suzanne Winter; to two families who kept me alive to write this book: The Hines family (I'll never go hungry with them around) and the Szeneri family (who has helped me in too many ways to try to list); to my good friend, Jan Szeneri—the poor soul God has designated my sounding board, and who lent me Calvin's commentaries on Moses since the U.S. Postal Service lost my set (sorry I had them so long); to John Calvin, an underappreciated ethicist; to mom, who has been telling me about Jesus as long as I can remember; and to my Lord, who supplied me with the above people, the desire to learn, and indeed, the very graces in Christ Jesus.

Introduction

Like the apostle Paul, who always attaches a "therefore" to his doctrines, John Calvin believed in an applicable theology, an *ethical* theology. As the resolute herald of *sola Scriptura*, he supplied his ethic with the norms of God's Word, including those norms given through Moses' hand; indeed, "Biblical law served the basis of Calvin's ethics."[1] So adamant was he that the Law is integral to morality, he wrote, "any zeal for good works that wanders outside God's law is an intolerable profanation of divine and true righteousness."[2]

With this moral system, Calvin and his followers conquered their worlds. The moral details of Mosaic revelation gave them a great edge over their rivals, propelling them into the lead of their cultures. While others remained in dark confusion, Calvinists followed a clear route, lit by script that boasts itself a lamp unto feet and a light unto paths. And since godliness holds promise for this life (Deut 28:1–2; 1 Tim 4:8), Calvin's Law-ethic brought with it great prosperity. "To urge us in every way," he would so often teach, "[God] promises both blessings in the present life and everlasting blessedness to those who obediently keep his commandments."[3] Wherever his influence spread, therefore, industry and education increased, idolatry decreased, ecclesiastical and political governments were well-ordered, and freedom abounded. One historian writes: "The principles which underlay Calvin's theological and ecclesiastical system have been a powerful factor in the growth of civil liberty."[4] In fact, opposing arbitrary kingly power and deposing political tyrants have conspicuously marked the followers of Calvin's ethic.[5]

---

1. Gary North, Publisher's Preface to *Covenant Enforced*, xi.
2. Calvin, *Institutes*, 2.8.5.
3. Calvin, *Institutes*, 2.8.4.
4. Fisher, *History*, 329.
5. In addition to Fisher's book, see: Douglas F. Kelly, *The Emergence of Liberty in the Modern World: The Influence of Calvin on Five Governments from the 16th Through 18th Centuries* (Phillipsburg, NJ: P & R, 1992); Nathaniel S. McFetridge, *Calvinism in*

The Encyclopedia Britannica sums it up well: "The Calvinist form of Protestantism is widely thought to have had a major impact on the formation of the modern world."[6]

Modern American Christendom, though, in throwing out the Mosaic Law, undoes what the followers of Calvin have accomplished. It should come as no surprise that in a day when a popular theologian teaches "the Mosaic Law ended with the first advent of Christ,"[7] a major magazine reports that "Christians are now making up a declining percentage of the American population."[8] Christianity's lack of influence on this country correlates with the lack of influence of the Law of Moses on Christianity.

The present volume, summarizing Calvin's commentaries on the Law of Moses, intends to reverse this trend. Understanding the will of the Lord, especially the detailed Mosaic portion,[9] is prerequisite to making the nations Christ's disciples. For as Christ makes teaching his commandments essential to this discipleship (Matt 28:20), Paul believed Christ's commandments included Mosaic instructions. So though his apostle could pull rank to settle moral questions (see 1 Cor 7:12; 14:37), he also had the option to simply declare "it is written in the law of Moses" (1 Cor 9:9). This volume, then, though a summary of Calvin's interpretation of Moses, also follows Paul as Paul followed Christ.

History: A Political, Moral and Evangelizing Force (Presbyterian Board of Publication, 1882; reprint, Birmingham, AL: Solid Ground Christian Books, 2004); A. Mervyn Davies, *Foundation of American Freedom* (New York: Abingdon, 1955); Rev. W.P. Breed, D.D., *Presbyterians and the Revolution* (Trustees of the Presbyterian Board of Publication, 1876; new ed., Powder Springs, GA: American Vision, 2008).

6. *Encyclopedia Britannica*, s.v. "Calvin and Calvinism," 15:450.

7. Ryrie, *Dispensationalism*, 57.

8. Meacham, "End of Christian America."

9. God reveals his will through his Word, even that portion written by Moses. David and Paul clearly equate the Law with God's will (Ps 40:8; Rom 2:18). Though God has a secret will whereby he providentially causes all things (Eph 1:11), he also has a *revealed* will that he expects us to follow: "The secret things belong to the LORD our God, but those things which are revealed belong to us and to our children forever, that we may do all the words of this law" (Deut 29:29). Here Moses equates God's Law to his revealed will—the revelation of his *moral* will for our lives. Calvin did the same: "it is the perfection of a good and holy life, when we live in obedience to his will. . . . that will which is made known in the Law" (*Commentaries*, Heb 13:21). Elsewhere God's will is equated with Paul's commandments (1 Thess 4:2–3) and with good works (Col 1:9–10; Heb 13:21), and contrasted with fleshly and lustful living (1 Pet 4:2; 1 John 2:17).

STRUCTURE OF THIS BOOK

Calvin skillfully systematized his commentaries on Exodus through Deuteronomy.[10] He begins with the first chapter of Exodus, with Israel in Egypt. He continues like any ordinary commentary, moving successively by chapter and verse, covering Israel's history until they arrive at Mount Sinai. From there he stops the historical exposition and begins a systematic teaching on the Ten Commandments, rounding up all Mosaic laws under their respective Decalogical commandments, and then expounds each law.

This book summarizes Calvin's systematic exposition of the laws of Moses. One of its aims is to give Christians a rapid education in ethics. Whereas Calvin's exposition covers over eight hundred pages, this summary covers only a few hundred. Its bullet-point format further expedites the education; concise information takes priority over rhetorical flourish.

Each chapter deals with one of the Ten Commandments, and typically covers:

(1) *General Principle*.[11] Each of the Ten Commandments teaches a general principle, but each conveys the principle by synecdoche; that is, the law specified is a part standing for a whole class of laws. For example, the sixth commandment reads "You shall not murder," but the general principle is, "We must not vex, oppress, or hate anyone." "You shall not murder" is a particular law standing for a whole class of laws forbidding vexations, oppressions, and hatred. Explaining why God might have chosen to present the Decalogue this way, Calvin writes:

> God has set forth by way of example the most frightful and wicked element in every kind of transgression, at the hearing of which our senses might shudder, in order that he might imprint upon our minds a greater detestation of every sort of sin. . . . For example, when called by their own names, we do not consider anger and hatred as things to be cursed. Yet when they are forbidden under the name "murder," we better understand how abominable they are in the sight of God, by whose Word they are relegated to the level of a dreadful crime.[12]

---

10. Calvin, *Commentaries on the Four Last Books of Moses*.

11. Though Calvin does not include General Principle headers in his commentaries, they have been added to assist the reader.

12. Calvin, *Institutes*, 2.8.10.

Each header, furthermore, retains the positive or negative wording of the Ten Commandments. If the commandment reads, "You shall," the header is stated positively; if "You shall not," the header is stated negatively. Calvin reminds us, though, that "in negative precepts, . . . the opposite affirmation is also to be understood."[13] So the sixth commandment does not simply prohibit oppressions, it also positively affirms "the requirement that we give our neighbor's life all the help we can."[14]

(2) *Decalogue law*. In the sixth commandment, for instance, Calvin first interprets the Decalogical law "You shall not murder."

(3) *Exposition*. These case laws illustrate how the general principle taught in that Decalogical law applies in various situations. For example, Calvin considers "You shall not curse the deaf, nor put a stumbling block before the blind" (Lev 19:14) as a particular case law that illustrates, or gives an "exposition" of, the principle taught in the sixth commandment. Cursing the deaf and tripping the blind are cases of oppression.

(4) *Political supplemental laws* (if applicable). Lastly, Calvin collects and interprets political supplements, or aids, to the commandments. With the sixth commandment again, he regards Leviticus 24:17—"Whoever kills any man shall surely be put to death"—as aiding political authorities to handle murder.

USES OF THIS BOOK

One may use this volume, first, as a *reference guide*. When encountering a difficult law in Moses' writings, simply refer to the Scripture index to locate the page in this volume discussing that law. Or perhaps you need ethical guidance about a particular matter. Knowing that the Ten Commandments are ten perspectives on *all* of life, simply read the chapter of the Decalogical law dealing with the matter in question. Suppose, for instance, the matter concerns what to do about a stray dog that has appeared on your front porch, whom your children desire to keep. Since the matter concerns property, and knowing that the eighth commandment deals with property (let the "General Principle" headers help you here), reading through the chapter on the eighth commandment will bring you across Deuteronomy 22:1–3 and Exodus 23:4. These verses will guide you to make a righteous decision about the dog.

---

13. Calvin, *Commentaries*, Exod 20:13; Deut 5:17.
14. Calvin, *Institutes*, 2.8.9.

Using this book as a reference guide, though, involves research *after* a question arises. For the more initiated students, who prepare themselves for questions *before* they emerge (Prov 15:28), this volume can also be used for an *expedited ethics education*. In a sense, these few hundred pages cover the entirety of moral instruction. For though the Scriptures sufficiently supply us with moral direction, *completely* training us in righteousness and equipping us for *every* good work (2 Tim 3:16–17), the Mosaic revelation occupies a unique place in Scripture. Concerning ethics, it is the seed from which the rest of the Scriptures blossom. As Calvin rightly teaches, the new oracles of the prophets added to the Old Testament (i.e., the books of Joshua through Malachi) were "not so new that they did not flow from the law and hark back to it. As for doctrine, they were only interpreters of the law and added nothing to it except predictions of things to come. Apart from these, they brought nothing forth but a pure exposition of the law."[15] Likewise with the relationship between the Old Testament and the writings of the apostles: "so far as relates to the substance, nothing has been added; for the writings of the apostles contain nothing else than a simple and natural explanation of the Law and the Prophets."[16] Consequently, all moral revelation traces back to that Scripture written with God's own finger (Exod 31:18; Deut 9:10), causing Calvin to say confidently: "nothing can be wanted as the rule of a good and upright life beyond the Ten Commandments."[17] Reading this book from cover to cover, then, *quickly* educates one in ethics.

COMPETITORS TO THIS BOOK

The state of modern theology calls for an analysis of two competitors to Calvin. Since Antinomianism and Natural Law dominate Christendom, and since without a proper dismissal of these ideas, Calvin's Law-ethic may remain in doubt, a somewhat brief critique of each follows.

---

15. Calvin, *Institutes*, 4.8.6.
16. Calvin, *Commentaries*, 2 Tim 3:17.
17. Calvin, "Preface of John Calvin to the Four Last Books of Moses," xvii.

Antinomianism

DISPENSATIONAL VERSION

Unlike Calvin, many theologians today make themselves ethically unhelpful by lopping off the Mosaic portion of the Lord's Word. They have *antinomian* (i.e., against the Law) tendencies at least toward this portion of God's Law.[18] They rely heavily on passages such as Galatians 3:24–25, "Therefore the law was our tutor to bring us to Christ, that we might be justified by faith. But after faith has come, we are no longer under a tutor"; Romans 10:4, "For Christ is the end of the law"; and especially Romans 6:14, "for you are not under law but under grace."[19] From these they reason that Moses' statutes are morally irrelevant to the New Covenant Christian:

> The specific provisions of the Mosaic law in Exodus–Deuteronomy were intended to apply directly only to Israel at that time.[20]

> Simply put, the New Testament explicitly presents the Old Testament Mosaic law in its entirety as abrogated and replaced by a similar law, the law of Christ, which places greater premium on dependence on the indwelling Holy Spirit.[21]

> The entire Mosaic law comes to fulfillment in Christ, and this fulfillment means that this law is no longer a *direct and immediate* source of, or judge of, the conduct of God's people. Christian behavior, rather, is now guided directly by "the law of Christ."[22]

From these quotes, though, we see that they do not leave us without ethical guidance. They are not antinomian in the sense of allowing anarchy or unrestraint. There is still a law for the New Covenant believer, the Law of Christ. This law is the New Testament's codification of the eternal

---

18. God's *Law* includes all of God's Word from Genesis to Revelation. "The Law" sometimes refers to the five books of Moses (Matt 5:17; Luke 16:16; 24:44; Rom 3:21b), sometimes to the entire Old Testament (Matt 5:18; John 10:34; 15:25; Rom 3:19; 1 Cor 14:21), and sometimes to the entire Bible (Isa 2:3; Jas 1:22–25). Accordingly, all of Scripture is useful for ethical instruction (Rom 15:4; 1 Cor 10:11; 2 Tim 3:16–17), every single word (Deut 8:3; Matt 4:4).

19. Other passages used are 2 Cor 3; Phil 3:7–9.

20. Grudem, *Politics*, 84; cf. 27, 66, 192. See my review of Grudem's book at www.annodomini.co.

21. Strickland, *Five Views*, 163; cf. 276.

22. Moo, *Five Views*, 343; cf. 346.

moral law of God. The Law of Moses was one codified form; the Law of Christ is its newer codified form. Therefore:

> We should approach the New Testament with the assumption that whatever is not re-introduced and re-instated in the New Covenant is no longer in effect.[23]

> We are bound only to that [of the Mosaic law] which is clearly repeated within New Testament teaching.[24]

The code found in Moses was tailored to that specific people for that specific time. Thus, "While there is unity between the Testaments when it comes to moral directives [eternal moral principles], there is diversity between the Testaments when it comes to ethical directions [cultural applications of the eternal principles]."[25] We know what laws of the Old Testament are eternal by their reintroduction into the New Testament. This, then, is one form of antinomianism, what one theologian called "*dispensational* antinomianism."[26]

LATENT VERSION

Another form, "*latent* antinomianism,"[27] does not say that Christ ended all of Moses' Law, but only certain laws. John Murray asked, "Are we not compelled to recognize that the New Testament . . . institutes a change from one set of canons to another, and that therefore there is not only development and addition, but reversal and abrogation?"[28] The laws in which these theologians particularly find cessation are the civil laws: "It is conceivable that the progress of revelation would remove the necessity for the penal sanction. This is the case with the death penalty for adultery. And the same holds true for many other penal sanctions of

23. Morey, *Relate*, 144.
24. Moo, *Five Views*, 376; cf. 172.
25. Morey, *Relate*, 42.
26. Bahnsen, *By This Standard*, 299. "This form of antinomianism is called 'dispensational' because it stands opposed to the law of the previous dispensation (the Old Covenant law of Moses)," 299–300.
27. Bahnsen, *By This Standard*, 301. Though the word "antinomian" sometimes carries a pejorative connotation, nothing accusatory is meant here; it is simply a convenient label for these schools of thought. I suppose Calvin and I would be "antinomian" to Orthodox Jews for not holding to Old Covenant ceremonial laws (according to Col 2:17; Heb 10:1 et al.).
28. Murray, *Principles of Conduct*, 15.

the Mosaic economy."²⁹ "Such provisions of the Mosaic law," Murray explains elsewhere, "are so closely bound up with an economy which has passed away as to its observance, that we could hold to the continuance of these provisions no more than we could hold to the continuance of the Mosaic economy itself."³⁰ Willem A. VanGemeren likewise teaches that the "civil laws, and the penal code have been abrogated."³¹

The rationale for singling out the civil laws varies. As Murray said above, sometimes these laws are said to be uniquely tied to ancient Israel.³² Sometimes the additional revelation and greater working of the Spirit in the New Covenant make such severe punishments now unnecessary.³³ Still other times a cleavage is made between the moral law and the civil law.³⁴ Since "the moral law of God . . . was based on the character of God,"³⁵ it remains; the civil law was not, therefore it vanishes.

Critique of Dispensational Version

Antinomianism's failure should not surprise the biblical student. If the granting of the Law was gracious (Ps 119:29), what should we consider its abrogation? As the New Covenant exceeds the graciousness of the Old Covenant, we should not expect the New to abrogate the Mosaic Law. But beyond this prima facie problem, other difficulties confront Antinomianism.

First, the Dispensational version allows what most would consider atrocious acts. According to it, God has eternal principles that have differing outward codified forms, and believers are only obliged to that form under which they live. Moo puts it this way: "Indeed, we can confidently expect that everything within the Mosaic law that reflected God's 'eternal moral will' for his people is caught up into and repeated in the 'law of Christ.'"³⁶ In other words, if a law is not repeated in the New Covenant, it is not God's eternal law nor binding on today's believer.

---

29. Murray, *Principles of Conduct*, 118; cf. 54, 119 and *Collected Writings*, 1:211–212.
30. Murray, *Collected Writings*, 1:211–212.
31. Willem A. VanGemeren, *Five Views*, 37.
32. Murray, *Collected Writings*, 1:211–212; cf. VanGemeren, *Five Views*, 53, 148.
33. Murray, *Collected Writings*, 1:212. *Principles of Conduct*, 118.
34. Walter C. Kaiser Jr., *Five Views*, 189–190. VanGemeren, *Five Views*, 148.
35. Kaiser, *Five Views*, 190.
36. Moo, *Five Views*, 370.

But when we think about what Mosaic commandments are not repeated in the New Covenant, we wonder if Dispensationalism is serious about this hermeneutic. The law prohibiting sexual relations with your sister (Lev 18:9) is not repeated. Is this then now morally permissible? Statutes forbidding tripping blind people or cursing deaf people (Lev 19:14) are not repeated. Are we then free in Christ to trip and curse? Mosaic laws banning cross-dressing (Deut 22:5) and sexual relations with animals (Lev 18:23) find no place in the New Testament. Does the Law of Christ permit dressing as the opposite sex and having relations with beasts? Undoubtedly, Dispensationalists *personally* repudiate these practices; nevertheless, their *interpretation scheme* allows them.[37]

Second, Dispensationalism misunderstands the characteristics of the Law of Moses, and for this reason sees a great discontinuity between the ethic promulgated by Moses and the New Covenant ethic. This becomes obvious from Moo's description of the New Covenant ethic:

> The law of Christ "stands in Paul's thought for those 'prescriptive principles stemming from the heart of the gospel (usually embodied in the example and teachings of Jesus), which are meant to be applied to specific situations by the direction and enablement of the Holy Spirit, being always motivated and conditioned by love.'"[38]

This description of the Law of Christ contains five characteristics. However, each characteristic equally applies to the Mosaic Law:

(1) *"Prescriptive principles stemming from the heart of the gospel..."* In Romans 10:6–8, the apostle Paul quotes a passage from Moses (Deut 30:12–14) and then says that Moses here preached the same gospel as he preached. The Mosaic prescriptive principles stem from the heart of the gospel.

(2) *"... usually embodied in the example and teachings of Jesus..."* Jesus lived according to Mosaic principles (Matt 4:4, 7, 10 quoting Deut 6:13, 16; 8:3). He also teaches the Mosaic ethic in his own ministry:

---

37. For a convincing critique of Dispensationalism, see *The Bahnsen/Feinberg Debate—The Place of O.T. Law on the Life of the N.T. Believer*, available from *Covenant Media Foundation* (mp3 audio), http://www.cmfnow.com/search.aspx?find=Bahnsen%2fFeinberg+Debate.

38. Moo, *Five Views*, 369. Moo is approvingly quoting Richard N. Longenecker, *Galatians* (Dallas: Word, 1990), 275-276, where Longenecker is quoting from one of his (Longenecker's) own previous books.

citing "Do not defraud" (Mark 10:19), which is the ethical principle of Deuteronomy 25:4 (see Luke 10:7; 1 Tim 5:18); and commanding his audience to "love your enemies" (Matt 5:44), echoing the instructions of Moses in Exodus 23:4–5. Jesus' example and teachings embody the laws of Moses.

(3) "*. . . which are meant to be applied to specific situations . . .*" In Matthew 15:4, Jesus quotes the Mosaic prescriptive principle of honoring parents (Exod 20:12), and then quotes a Mosaic application of that principle (Exod 21:17; Lev 20:9). The Mosaic principles are meant to be applied to specific situations.

(4) "*. . . by the direction and enablement of the Holy Spirit . . .*" Obedience to the Law of Moses always required the Spirit's power (Ezek 36:27; Rom 8:4). How else could Old Covenant saints like Joshua, David, and Daniel, whose natures were no less sinful than ours, have obeyed God's laws?

(5) "*. . . being always motivated and conditioned by love.*" Love has always been the motivation to obey God, even during the Mosaic administration (Lev 19:18, 34; Deut 6:5; 10:12).

A proper understanding of the Law of Moses, therefore, shows it to have identical characteristics to the Law of Christ. Second Timothy 3:16–17 buttresses this conclusion. Since here Paul ascribes moral *sufficiency* to the Old Testament Scriptures, New Testament revelation could only *reiterate* Old Testament moral teachings.

In addition to allowing atrocious acts and misunderstanding Moses' Law, Dispensationalism is subject to a third criticism: it misunderstands the New Testament phrase "Law of Christ," not recognizing it as *mediation terminology*. For once Christ faithfully accomplished his earthly ministry, New Testament writers joyfully attach his title to well-known, well-established phrases. For example, all men are created as the image of God (Gen 1:26; Jas 3:9), and yet Paul speaks of our redemption as conformity to the image *of Christ* (Rom 8:29; 1 Cor 15:49)—should we conclude that Paul speaks of another image altogether? Should we not rather understand Paul as using mediation terminology, that is, language emphasizing Christ's mediatorial work in redeeming us back to God's righteous image?

Here is another example: Christ is a mediatorial King. As uniquely God and man, he alone may mediate between God and man (1 Tim 2:5).

As divine, kingly rule intrinsically belongs to him, but as the mediatorial God-man, this rule is *bestowed* on him. In other words, Christ, because of his obedience to the Father (John 10:18), secured this rule (Isa 53:11–12; Phil 2:8–9; Heb 2:9). Whereas God reigns over all (Ps 103:19), setting over mankind those magistrates whom he wills (Dan 5:21), and this in virtue of his creation (Jer 27:5–6), the mediatorial rule of Christ is "given" (Dan 7:14; Matt 28:18), "bestowed" (Luke 22:29), and "delivered" (Matt 11:27) to him by the Father. It takes place at a particular time.[39] Therefore, God's intrinsic rule and Christ's mediatorial rule are *formally different*, and yet they are *materially identical*, that is, the people and bounds over which they rule are the same.[40] God now mediates his kingdom through the Messiah. Consequently, we should not infer from the expression "kingdom of Christ" (Eph 5:5;[41] cf. Col 1:13) that Christ rules over different people and different bounds than does the Father, any more than we should understand that a different Spirit is spoken of because in one place he is called the "Spirit *of God*" (Gen 1:2) and in others the "Spirit *of Christ*" (Rom 8:9;[42] 1 Pet 1:11). Alternate lingo must not derail proper theology.

Likewise, we should not infer two different law structures from two different designations. As with all kings, Christ rules his kingdom by way of laws. He reigns over all the peoples of the earth (Ps 2:8; Dan 7:14) by his righteous law (Isa 2:3–4; 11:4; 2 Thess 2:8; Rev 19:15, 21). It is the sword he wields to reclaim his rightful domain; it is the rod that brooks no compromise. About this, nineteenth century Covenanter pastor William Symington writes:

> *Laws* are essential to dominion; it cannot exist long without them; and there can be no administration where they are entirely

---

39. Though at the birth of Jesus, he was declared a king (Matt 2:2; cf. Isa 9:6–7), and though his preaching was of a kingdom "at hand" (Matt 4:17; 10:7; Mark 1:14–15), and though he forcefully proclaimed that by exorcizing demons "the kingdom of God has come upon you" (Matt 12:28), these were but anticipatory of Jesus' actual inauguration. They crescendoed the loud clash of his glorious resurrection. Christ occupied his throne when death could no longer hold him (Acts 2:30–31). And at his ascension, thereafter, when in the flesh beholding his Father, he was given his everlasting kingdom (Dan 7:13–14). From that enthronement he rules in the midst of his enemies, progressively making them his footstool (Ps 110:1–2; Eph 1:20–23; Heb 10:12–13).

40. Symington, *Messiah the Prince*, 67.

41. This verse even runs together "the kingdom of Christ and God."

42. This verse actually interchanges the "Spirit of God" and the "Spirit of Christ."

wanting. The Messiah is not without these; the Scriptures are the law of the Lord—a code at once righteous, suitable, extensive, and efficacious.[43]

Therefore, the "Law of Christ" (1 Cor 9:21;[44] Gal 6:2) bears the same content as the Law of God. As the Law of God includes those laws given through Moses, so also does the Law of Christ. They differ only in name. The law of God's kingdom can now bear the name of the King through whom God mediates his rule. Consequently, in regards to moral teaching, the Law of Christ *is* the Law of Moses.

Critique of Latent Version

The latent form of Antinomianism fares little better. First, it reasons poorly to separate the civil laws from the moral law. Walter C. Kaiser Jr. gives a number of passages to show that the moral aspects of the law take priority over the ceremonial *and civil* aspects.[45] However, these passages only show so with regard to the ceremonial laws. In 1 Samuel 15:22-23, for instance, moral laws are set over burnt offerings, sacrifices, and the fat of rams. In Isaiah 1:11-17, moral laws are set against sacrifices; burnt offerings of rams; the fat of cattle; offering the blood of bulls, lambs, goats; incense; and new moon and Sabbath feasts. These passages say nothing of civil ordinances, but only ceremonial ones. The same is true of the other passages that Kaiser cites (Jer 7:21-23; Mic 6:8; Ps 51:16-17).[46] And Murray is certain that the death penalty continues to exist for murder, while agnostic about its applicability to other crimes,[47] but then acknowledges the New Testament's teaching that crimes (plural!) merit the death penalty.[48]

Moreover, Latent Antinomianism arbitrarily sets apart the civil laws from the moral law. Theologians commonly categorize the laws of the Old Testament into moral, ceremonial, and civil categories. But why

---

43. Symington, *Messiah the Prince*, 17.
44. This verse actually equates the "law of God" and the "law of Christ."
45. Kaiser, *Five Views*, 189-190.
46. Kaiser's position involves another difficulty when he says that "the civil and ceremonial laws functioned only as further illustrations of the moral law" (*Five Views*, 190). Does he really believe that the ceremonial laws were of a like kind ("illustrations") with the moral laws? Or that the civil laws functioned similarly to the ceremonial laws?
47. Murray, *Principles of Conduct*, 118-122.
48. Murray, *Principles of Conduct*, 120.

are the civil laws singled out from the moral laws? Why are never the familial laws, or economic laws, or ecclesiastical laws singled out? Why is there never a category scheme of moral, ceremonial, *and familial*? Because theologians recognize the Mosaic familial laws as simply those moral laws applicable to the family. They should recognize the same concerning the civil laws; they are those moral laws applicable to the civil realm. And so if the civil laws are part of the moral law, they are based on the eternal character of God and therefore continue to obligate in the New Covenant.[49]

Second, the New Testament expressly endorses the civil laws of Moses. Not only are they *generally* endorsed by Jesus' and Paul's comments (Matt 5:16–20; 2 Tim 3:16–17), but the New Testament *particularly* endorses them as well. Writing to Timothy, Paul emphasizes the political use of the Law (1 Tim 1:8–10). Certain laws of God, he says, are "not made for a righteous person" (i.e., the law-abiding citizen), but are for restraining the "lawless and insubordinate" persons in society. He gives some examples of the kinds of behavior God's Law considers criminal: killing parents, murder, prostitution or adultery or bestiality, homosexuality, kidnapping, and lying and perjury.[50] This political use of the Law, Paul assures us, is a "good" and "lawful" use (v. 8). For every penalty given by Moses, the writer to the Hebrews informs us, is "a *just* penalty" (Heb 2:2, NASB)—they are expressions of God's moral standards of justice. So the civil penalty prescribed, say, for homosexuality (Lev 20:13) is an ordinance of perfect *justice*, and for this reason Paul recognizes homosexuality as worthy of civil punishment (Rom 1:32).[51]

---

49. Being *moral*, then, the civil laws apply to all peoples throughout all times. Recognizing this truth answers the teaching that the Mosaic civil laws were uniquely applicable to ancient Israel. Cf. Murray, *Collected Writings*, 1:211–212 and VanGemeren, *Five Views*, 53, 148.

50. Some of the passages Paul probably has in mind are Exod 21:12, 15, 16; 22:19; Lev 20:10, 13, 15–16; 24:17; Deut 19:15–21; 22:13–24; 24:7.

51. The phrase "deserving of death" in Scripture always refers to capital punishment by the State (e.g., Deut 17:6; 19:6; 21:22; Luke 23:15; Acts 23:29); it is this "righteous judgment of God" to which Paul refers. Additionally, the "such things" of Romans 1:32 refer to the homosexual practices listed back in vv. 26–27. The sins listed in the intermediary verses (vv. 28–31) are those that so often attend a society that openly embraces homosexual practices. Bahnsen nicely summarizes the syntax of the passage: "'Being filled with' in Rom 1:29 modifies 'them' in Rom 1:28, which is to say, the homosexuals of Rom 1:26, 27" (*Homosexuality*, 59n.113). Frame writes similarly: "Afterward [after Romans 1:24–27], Paul lists other sins that result from unbelief (vv. 28–32). But among all the sins listed in

Moreover, in Matthew 15:3–6, Jesus rebukes the Pharisees and scribes for allowing their traditions to override the civil punishments listed in the Pentateuch (Exod 21:17; Lev 20:9). And lastly, when Paul stands before the tribunal of Governor Festus, he recognizes crimes (plural) that are deserving of death (Acts 25:8–11)—crimes involving capital offenses according to *Jewish* laws (Acts 23:29; 24:6)—a recognition he certainly would not have made for unjust penal laws.

So contrary to the claims of Latent Antinomianism, the civil punishments listed in God's Law have not terminated. As criminal behavior has not ceased in the New Covenant era, God has not ended his ordained means of dealing with crime. Indeed, Romans 12:19—13:4 teaches us that civil rulers are the servants *of God*, who do "not bear the sword in vain" (13:4) but have been appointed to execute *his* wrath upon evil doers; and God by no means leaves it up to man to determine what his wrath might be. Additionally, the requirement of penal precision (Prov 17:15; Deut 17:20) makes adhering to God's instructions absolutely necessary. Calvin's words are right on target: "And this is worthy of observation, that those who are armed with the sword, must not go out of the way on either side one tittle, but faithfully execute whatever God prescribes."[52] All of Scripture, even God's civil penalties, is useful for ethical instruction (2 Tim 3:16–17). Throwing out that portion of Scripture given to instruct us in the punishment of criminals is done to our own peril, as the evening news and overcrowded jails daily declare. The ancient sage must have seen our day when he wrote: "Where there is no revelation [of God], the people cast off restraint" (Prov 29:18).

Antinomianism, we have seen, falls to the ground. Not only does it allow atrocious acts, but its attempts at invalidating Old Testament laws spring from a misunderstanding of both the Law of Moses and the Law of Christ. Furthermore, its attempt to keep some laws but throw out others fails due to faulty reasoning and to an oversight of New Testament teaching. All Scripture is inspired of God, making its every word useful for ethical instruction (Matt 4:4; 2 Tim 3:16–17); every jot and tittle of Moses comes into the New Covenant (Matt 5:18) unless Christ says otherwise. Like the saints of old, we declare God's Law liberating (Jas 1:25; 2:12; cf. Ps 119:45) and life-giving (Matt 19:17; cf. Deut 4:1). The Christian's attitude should be that of the psalmist: "Oh, how I love Your law! It is my medita-

---

the chapter, homosexuality has a place of prominence" (*DCL*, 758).

52. Calvin, *Commentaries*, Num 31:14.

tion all the day" (Ps 119:97). We do not manifest maturity by ignoring the wisdom given to us by Omniscience. On the contrary, turning aside from *any* of God's commandments is to praise the wicked (Prov 28:4) and "to go after other gods to serve them" (Deut 28:14). If we heed our Lord's testimonies, we shall understand more than all of our teachers (Ps 119:99). Dear Christian, "keeping the commandments of God is what matters" (1 Cor 7:19), "for this is man's all" (Eccl 12:13).

Natural Law

Though Antinomianism seeks to ignore portions of God's Word, we now encounter a philosophy that makes all of God's Word unnecessary for ethical direction. Seeking an alternate route for moral guidance, Natural Law is defined as

> the moral order inscribed in the world and especially in human nature, an order that is known to all people through their natural faculties (especially reason and/or conscience) even apart from supernatural divine revelation that binds morally the whole of the human race.[53]

As critics have shown, though, the Natural Law ethic commits the naturalistic fallacy, erroneously moving from what *is* the case in nature to what morally *ought* to be the case. But what gives nature this kind of moral authority? Without authority, obligation cannot exist.

Some advocates of nature, however, appeal to the Bible and to the God of the Bible for this natural order's authority. J. Budziszewski, for example, says that "the Bible itself testifies to the reality of the natural law,"[54] and that Natural Law derives its "authority from God alone."[55] David VanDrunen teaches that "natural law need not be considered a godless or autonomous law—indeed, it should not be. . . . [T]he natural law is in fact given by God and bears its authority from him";[56] therefore

---

53. VanDrunen, *Biblical Case*, 1; cf. 14, 44, 49. J. Budziszewski defines it as the "moral principles that are both right for everybody and knowable to everybody by the ordinary exercise of human reason" (*Written on the Heart*, 109); and describes it thus: "*Natural* law . . . is built into the design of human nature and woven into the fabric of the normal human mind" ("Natural Law"). See my review of VanDrunen's book at www.annodomini.co.

54. Budziszewski, "Natural Law."

55. Budziszewski, *Written on the Heart*, 210.

56. VanDrunen, *Biblical Case*, 7.

"appealing to natural law . . . [is] ultimately to the authority of God the Creator."[57] So when Natural Law is defined as known "apart from supernatural divine revelation," what is meant is God's *verbal* revelation, whether spoken or written.[58]

But if these Natural theologians appeal to the Bible and to the God of the Bible to give authority to their ethic, why not seek the entire ethic from his Word? To this question they have at least two replies. First, a *common* ethical standard is needed for the common social and political realms enjoyed by both believers and unbelievers. "The character of the civil kingdom[59] as a common realm calls for a moral standard that is common to all human beings, and this is what natural law is."[60] Scripture's ethical guidance, on the other hand, is for believers only: "Biblical moral instructions are given to people who are redeemed and are given as a consequence of their redemption,"[61] and therefore, "Scripture is not the appropriate moral standard for the civil kingdom."[62] T. David Gordon concurs: "The Bible is sufficient to guide the human-as-covenanter, but not sufficient to guide the human-as-mechanic, the human-as-physician, the human-as businessman, the human-as-parent, the human-as-husband, the human-as-wife, or the human-as-legislator."[63] And discussing the topic of homosexuality, Budziszewski writes:

> Among activists who want to keep the "hetero" in "sexuality," a consensus is developing that we need a "public philosophy," a way to speak wisdom to the people. It is pretty much taken for granted that means something different from quoting Scripture to our fellow citizens; they don't all believe in the Bible, those who say they believe it interpret it in diverse ways, and they are suspicious of anything that looks like "forcing one's religious opinions upon others."[64]

---

57. VanDrunen, *Biblical Case*, 4.

58. Throughout *Biblical Case*, VanDrunen distinguishes Natural Law from "special revelation" (43, 63), "special divine revelation" (50–51, 53), "a sacred text" (43), and "Scripture" (65, 66).

59. "This civil kingdom pertains to temporal, earthly, provisional matters, not matters of ultimate and spiritual importance." VanDrunen, *Biblical Case*, 24.

60. VanDrunen, *Biblical Case*, 35.

61. VanDrunen, *Biblical Case*, 39.

62. VanDrunen, *Biblical Case*, 38.

63. Gordon, "Insufficiency of Scripture."

64. Budziszewski, Review of *Homosexuality and American*.

VanDrunen likewise asks, "And what if . . . my neighbor is not a Christian and does not accept Scripture as a moral authority? Do I tell her that if she does not submit to the Scriptures then she has no right to participate in the political process?"[65]

Second, they say the Bible itself endorses Natural Law. Budziszewski was quoted earlier as saying "the Bible itself testifies to the reality of the natural law."[66] VanDrunen, who titles his book *A Biblical Case for Natural Law*, says "that natural law is taught in Scripture and should be affirmed in Christian theology."[67] He notes "that when God's people [in the Bible] . . . interacted with others in the civil kingdom, they did so by appealing to a common, natural moral standard rather than to the particular special revelation divinely given to their covenant community."[68] He gives the examples of the pagan Abimelech, who believed that polyandry was simply a thing that should not be done (Gen 20:9); of Moses' father-in-law, Jethro, who advised that the fear of God should be a criterion for electing judges (Exod 18:21); and of Job, who was deterred from unjustly treating his slaves by considering the notion of a common humanity (Job 31:13–15).[69] In all of these examples, appeal is made to common moral notions, not to any word from God. Furthermore, Natural theologians claim that Paul's teaching of the law written on human hearts (Rom 2:14–15) "is a natural law because human nature itself proclaims this law and judges whether it has been kept."[70]

CRITIQUE: MISUNDERSTANDS SCRIPTURE'S COMMONALITY

Though Natural Law has a prestigious pedigree, Christians should nevertheless shun its teachings for three major reasons. First, it misunderstands the common obligation of God's Word. If natural theologians seek a common standard, they need look no further than Holy Writ. God's voice, recorded for us in the Scriptures, binds all—believer and unbeliever. In Leviticus 18, for example, after God enumerates specific laws for Israel, he explains that it was the pagans failure to keep these *same* laws that caused their ejection from the land (vv. 24–30; cf. Deut

65. VanDrunen, "Anxious Kloosterman."
66. Budziszewski, "Natural Law."
67. VanDrunen, *Biblical Case*, 2.
68. VanDrunen, *Biblical Case*, 41.
69. VanDrunen, *Biblical Case*, 42–54.
70. VanDrunen, *Biblical Case*, 19.

18:9–14). In prescribing to the Jews the civil penalty for blasphemy, God declares that his penalties are for the "stranger as well as him who is born in the land," for "you shall have the same law for the stranger and for one from your own country" (Lev 24:16, 22).

Consider also God's condemnation of pagan nations: for violations of the first commandment, God condemned Moab (Jer 48:13, 35), Babylon (Isa 14:13–20; 21:9; Jer 50:2; Hab 1:11), and Nineveh (Nah 1:14); of the second commandment, Babylon (Isa 21:9; Jer 50:2, 38; 51:17–18, 47, 52), Egypt (Ezek 30:13), and Nineveh (Nah 1:14); of the eighth commandment, Ammon (Jer 49:1), and Nineveh (Nah 3:1); and of the ninth commandment, Nineveh (Nah 3:1).

Likewise, the prophet Jeremiah speaks of the prosperity and adversity of nations—both for covenanted Israel and unbelieving nations—as dependent on their adherence to God's law (Jer 18:7–11; cf. Deut 28). Paul could therefore summarize that "all the world" is "under the law" (Rom 3:19). Indeed, God's "word" binds universal "man" (Deut 8:3; Matt 4:4).

Moreover, God's revelation in nature and his revelation in word are, ethically speaking, *identical*. He reveals himself through the created order (Ps 19:1; Rom 1:19–20), man (Gen 1:26–27), and his Word (cp. Rom 7:12 and Lev 11:44; John 17:25; Mark 10:18). Each medium reveals the same God. And since he is our moral ideal (Lev 19:2; Matt 5:48; 1 Pet 1:15–16), each medium reveals the same moral teaching as well. Calvin notes this often:

> We have taught that the knowledge of God, otherwise quite clearly set forth in the system of the universe and in all creatures, is nonetheless more intimately and also more vividly revealed in his Word.[71]

> And yet nothing is set down there [in Ps 145] that cannot be beheld in his creatures. Indeed, with experience as our teacher we find God just as he declares himself in his Word.[72]

> Now that inward law, which we have above described as written, even engraved, upon the hearts of all, in a sense asserts the very same things that are to be learned from the two Tables [of the Law].[73]

---

71. Calvin, *Institutes*, 1.10.1.
72. Calvin, *Institutes*, 1.10.2.
73. Calvin, *Institutes*, 2.8.1.

> It is a fact that the law of God which we call the moral law is nothing else than a testimony of natural law and of that conscience which God has engraved upon the minds of men.[74]

> [The Law] prescribes nothing which nature does not itself dictate to be most certain and most just, and which experience itself does not shew us to be more profitable, or more desirable than anything else.[75]

Throughout his writings, Calvin shows this with particular behaviors, such as familial love;[76] offering military peace to a city before besieging it;[77] jurisprudence procedures;[78] honoring the elderly;[79] laws of consanguinity;[80] the subjection of women to the authority of men;[81] and even the political order,[82] which includes the punishment of fornication and adultery,[83] and violations of the degrees of consanguinity.[84] According to Calvin, then, nature and the Bible speak with one voice on these moral issues.

Surprisingly, modern Natural Law ethicists acknowledge this truth. Commenting on Romans 2:14–15, VanDrunen writes: "Paul makes it clear that the requirements of this natural law are essentially the same as those of the law of Moses."[85] Budziszewski similarly says that Natural Law "merely repeat[s] in cursive a small part of what God had already written in great block letters," and that the law of conscience and the Law of Moses both define sin.[86]

So if the moral requirements in nature and in Scripture are the same, why must we restrict Scripture to believers? Whatever nature obliges on unbelievers, Scripture also obliges on them. Why would we expect these

---

74. Calvin, *Institutes*, 4.20.16.
75. Calvin, *Commentaries*, Deut 10:12.
76. Calvin, *Commentaries*, Num 35:19; Deut 28:53.
77. Calvin, *Commentaries*, Deut 20:10.
78. Calvin, *Commentaries*, Deut 17:6; 19:15.
79. Calvin, *Commentaries*, Lev 19:32.
80. Calvin, *Commentaries*, Lev 18:6.
81. Calvin, *Commentary*, 1 Cor 14:34.
82. Calvin, *Institutes*, 2.2.13.
83. Calvin, "Adultery and Its Penalty."
84. Calvin, *Commentaries*, Lev 20:11–12, 14, 17, 19–21.
85. VanDrunen, *Biblical Case*, 19.
86. Budziszewski, *Written on the Heart*, 180, 181.

requirements to lose their obligation on unbelievers once they are written down? So at the very least, Natural Law advocates should have no problem with teaching God's *biblical* demands to everybody.

Critique: Advocates a Perverted Ethic

The Bible teaches natural *revelation*, not natural *law*. By confusing these two distinct concepts,[87] the Natural Law ethic results in teaching a perverted ethic. God does indeed reveal himself through the natural created order and through the very makeup of man (see proof-texts above). This revelation of God and of his standards are "clearly seen, being understood" by all (Rom 1:20). Calvin says that "men cannot open their eyes without being compelled to see him"[88]—"even the most untutored and ignorant persons";[89] and concerning the human makeup, Calvin writes that "a sense of divinity is by nature engraven on human hearts."[90] But before generalizing too hastily,[91] Van Til reminds us that "Calvin makes a sharp distinction between the revelation of God to man and man's response to that revelation."[92] These two concepts vastly differ. It is one thing to say that nature reveals God's righteous requirements and therefore all men know them, it is another thing altogether to advocate men follow this natural revelation apart from God's Word.[93] Biblical authors knew better than to advocate the latter.

Consider the situation before the Fall. Even then God gives his authoritative interpretations of nature. He tells Adam who he is, that is, the very image of God (Gen 1:26–27). God declares to Adam his mission in life, that is, to have dominion over the earth (Gen 1:26, 28; 2:15). By the

---

87. Budziszewski equates Natural Law with general (i.e., natural) revelation (*Written on the Heart*, 180).

88. Calvin, *Institutes*, 1.5.1.

89. Calvin, *Institutes*, 1.5.2.

90. Calvin, *Institutes*, 1.4.4.

91. VanDrunen hastily reasons from these kinds of comments by Calvin to the conclusion that Calvin advocated Natural Law (*Biblical Case*, 3, 18–19).

92. Van Til in Bahnsen, *Van Til's Apologetic*, 194.

93. Recall VanDrunen's definition of natural law: "the moral order inscribed in the world and especially in human nature, an order that is known . . . *even apart from supernatural divine revelation*" (*Biblical Case*, 1, emphasis mine). By "supernatural divine revelation," he obviously refers to God's Word, not divine revelation through nature (*Biblical Case*, 43, 50–51, 53, 63, 65, 66).

tree of the knowledge of good and evil God explains to Adam how to accomplish this mission. Van Til writes:

> God *identifies* one tree among many in order to indicate to man his task on earth. Man's task is to cultivate the earth and subdue it. He can do so only if he thinks and acts in obedience to his Maker. So his obedience must be tested. . . . [H]e needs a special supernatural test at the outset. He needs to learn by way of one example what he is to do with all the facts of history.[94]

Man has never been left alone to interpret himself and the world around him. The need for the coordination of word and nature "is inherent in the human situation."[95] To separate the two will not only bear no fruit, but it reenacts the *sin* of Adam by interpreting nature (in his case, the tree) independently of God's Word.

Now after the Fall, now that our minds have become futile, darkened, ignorant, and blind (Eph 4:17–18), should we think that God's interpretations of nature are unnecessary? Let Calvin's reflections on man's fallen condition expose the folly of such a consideration: "the whole man is overwhelmed—as by a deluge—from head to foot, so that no part is immune from sin and all that proceeds from him is to be imputed to sin. As Paul says, all turnings of the thoughts to the flesh are enmities against God [Rom. 8:7], and are therefore death [Rom. 8:6]."[96]

As nature reveals things unregenerate men dislike (e.g., that they cannot cheat on their taxes; that they cannot have sexual relations outside of marriage) and even things they fear (e.g., God's wrath), they are motivated to intentionally misinterpret nature. Their psyche cannot allow them to construe it rightly; there is too much at stake. Therefore, they "suppress the truth"[97] (Rom 1:18), rationalizing and gerrymandering it, deceiving themselves *both* about the truth revealed in nature

---

94. Van Til in Bahnsen, *Van Til's Apologetic*, 204.
95. Van Til in Bahnsen, *Van Til's Apologetic*, 203.
96. Calvin, *Institutes*, 2.1.9.
97. Unregenerate man suppresses the teaching of Scripture as well. But, first, written information is much more difficult to pervert. Second, Scripture contains within itself its own corrective to misinterpretation—that is, the gospel comes with ethical instructions from the Bible. "Since natural revelation does not bring people to salvation, it cannot prevent its own distortion in the human heart" (Frame, "Is Natural Revelation Sufficient"). And wanting a hearing with unbelievers, advocates of Natural Law tend to eschew the gospel when teaching ethics.

and about their intention to deceive themselves.[98] They simply will not handle nature properly. Their resultant interpretations of nature are lies (Rom 1:25).[99] It cannot be otherwise, for the noetic effects of sin are total. As a result, natural revelation is given to us "in vain," says Calvin, for it can "in no way lead us into the right path."[100]

We must bear in mind, consequently, two truths: (1) fallen people gain a true knowledge of God from nature, but (2) they always pervert this knowledge. About these two, Calvin writes:

> John speaks in this sense: "The light still shines in the darkness, but the darkness comprehends it not" [John 1:5]. In these words both facts are clearly expressed. First, in man's perverted and degenerate nature some sparks still gleam. These show him to be a rational being, differing from brute beasts, because he is endowed with understanding. Yet, secondly, they show this light choked with dense ignorance, so that it cannot come forth effectively.[101]

So though "the knowledge of good and evil is indeed imprinted by nature on men,"[102] this knowledge, as Calvin says above, "cannot come forth effectively." Sin has not and cannot obliterate our knowledge of good and evil received through nature—natural theologians rightly teach

---

98. Therefore, teaching that all men *know* right and wrong from nature, as per definitions of Natural Law, greatly oversimplifies the biblical picture. Unregenerate man is also *ignorant* of these same truths (Acts 17:23, 30; Eph 4:18; 1 Pet 1:14). This ignorance cannot be toned down to a lack of *intimate* knowledge, for ignorance is a lack of *intellectual* knowledge. Nor can we mitigate this ignorance by saying men simply "pretend" to not know, or simply refuse to acknowledge or admit that they know these truths (as says Budziszewski, *Written on the Heart*, 182, 183, 209). Unbelievers actually convince themselves that they *do not know* these truths. This awkward psychology can be illustrated thus: Atheist Andy believes God's moral truths revealed through nature, but Andy does not believe that Andy believes these moral truths. Andy's first belief is about God's moral truths; Andy's second belief is about Andy himself. For a more complete account of self-deception's bearing on Christian apologetics, read Greg Bahnsen, "The Crucial Concept of Self-Deception in Presuppositional Apologetics," Covenant Media Foundation, http://www.cmfnow.com/articles/pa207.htm (accessed August 27, 2002).

99. Consequently, Christians must always be cautious about ethical philosophies wherein unbelievers are supportive, as when humanist Paul Kurtz supports Natural Law: "The humanist life stance thus has its grounding in nature and human nature" (*Living Without Religion*, 38).

100. Calvin, *Institutes*, 1.5.14.

101. Calvin, *Institutes*, 2.2.12.

102. Calvin, "The Use of the Law," in *Commentaries on the Four Last Books of Moses*.

this truth. Fallen men, however, "suppress the truth [gained from natural revelation] in unrighteousness" (Rom 1:18)—natural theologians do not consider the full implications of this truth.

The consequences of this suppression, thinks Calvin, are fatal for Natural Law: The unregenerate man, the man who ignores the Bible, is "inconsistent with every decision of reason, and alien to the duties of men";[103] "they quickly choked by their own depravity the seed of right knowledge, before it grew up to ripeness";[104] all of their undertakings, like the "liberal sciences, and acquaintance with languages, are in a manner profaned in every instance,"[105] so that "in all their reasoning faculties they miserably fail"; "men, by their own guidance, are led only to vanity and lies"; man's "mind is so completely overwhelmed by the thraldom of ignorance, that any portion of *light* which remains in it is quenched and useless"; "all their understanding is nothing else than mere vanity"; "conscience perverts every decision, so as to confound vice with virtue"; and any knowledge they have for regulating their lives "passes away without yielding any advantage."[106] Man's natural knowledge is, in a word, morally worthless. Natural Law's failure to be a viable mechanism for ethical living causes Calvin to declare forthrightly, "The purpose of natural law,[107] therefore, is to render man inexcusable."[108] In other words, it functions negatively to take away man's excuse of ignorance (Rom 1:20), not positively as an independent moral guide.

And though natural theologians recognize man's proclivities to pervert natural revelation, incredibly they still encourage men to approach

---

103. Calvin, *Commentaries*, Rom 1:28.

104. Calvin, *Commentaries*, Rom 1:21.

105. Calvin, *Commentary*, 1 Cor 1:20.

106. Calvin, *Commentary*, John 1:5.

107. By "natural law" Calvin clearly means what I have called natural *revelation*. He goes on in this same passage to define what he means by natural law: "This would not be a bad definition: natural law is that apprehension of the conscience which distinguishes sufficiently between just and unjust, and which deprives men of the excuse of ignorance, while it proves them guilty by their own testimony." Thus, while Calvin states that fallen men gain an accurate knowledge of God from nature, there is no advocacy to follow nature apart from Scripture.

108. Calvin, *Institutes*, 2.2.22. VanDrunen suggests the same thing: "Perhaps [Paul's] primary point [in Rom 1:18–32] is that rebellious man is *inexcusable* before the judgment of God" (*Biblical Case*, 17). Again, I am bewildered that natural theologians can recognize these truths and yet not see the disastrous consequences these truths have for Natural Law.

nature alone: "There is a natural sense of rightness and wrongness that resides in the conscience (Rom. 2:14–15). Although this sense of right and wrong has been effaced by sin (1:32), it is nevertheless able to serve as the moral guide."[109] But can it serve as a moral guide to those whose sense of right and wrong has been "effaced"? VanDrunen admits that "man still knows [natural law], though in a corrupted fashion" and "Sinful human beings will constantly pervert and reject the teaching of natural law."[110] But should we advance a "corrupted" and "perverted" ethic? And though Budziszewski admits that unregenerate man suppresses God's revelation in nature, he never explains how they can *properly* handle it; he simply says that they know it.[111] But should we encourage men to follow a suppressed and mishandled revelation? We see then, by divorcing word and nature—separating what God has joined together—natural theology, in effect, advocates a depraved ethic.

Conversely, the Lord's sacred Word demands the Lord's sacred Word for ethics. Overcoming men's depravity requires the corrective gospel. Nature reveals to the sinner the *wrath* of God (Rom 1:18), not redemptive grace. Sinful man finds God's saving message solely in his Word (Rom 10:14–17). Also, God's Word objectively checks our interpretations of nature. "Man's Creator has provided the linguistic framework for 'exegeting' the truth of God in natural revelation and in man himself."[112] So though natural ethicists mean well when they counsel us to follow our hearts, the Lord notifies us that "he who trusts in his own heart is a fool" (Prov 28:26), for our hearts deceive us all too easily (Jer 17:9). Consequently, God bids us to follow his commandments so that we will not follow the perversions of our nature (Num 15:39), even as Jethro knew that his advice to Moses should only be followed if God approved (Exod 18:23).

When men do not filter their experiences through God's Word (*a la* Deut 6:6, 8), their studies of nature teach that same-sex civil unions should

---

109. Strickland, *Five Views*, 164.

110. VanDrunen, *Biblical Case*, 16, 40. He even advocates hearing unbelieving interpretations of nature for ecclesiastical and spiritual matters (67).

111. Budziszewski, "Natural Law."

112. Bahnsen, *Van Til's Apologetic*, 195. Calvin famously illustrated that using Scripture to read natural revelation is like an old bleary-eyed man putting on spectacles to read distinctly a beautiful book (*Institutes*, 1.6.1).

be recognized by the civil authorities,[113] or that all marital sexual relations be "ordered *per se* to the procreation of human life,"[114] or that sheepherding is a loathsome profession (Gen 46:34), or that men who survive snake bites are gods (Acts 28:3–6). Foolishness inevitably results from theories not founded on Christ's rock-words (Matt 7:24–27). "Yet hence it appears," agrees Calvin, "that if men were taught only by nature, they would hold to nothing certain or solid or clear-cut, but would be so tied to confused principles as to worship an unknown god [cf. Acts 17:23]."[115]

CRITIQUE: TENDS TO IDOLATRY

To understand this third criticism we must understand authority-hierarchies. In life we obey many authorities, ranging from personal authorities like fathers, policemen, teachers, and employers to impersonal authorities like sense perception, our faculties (rational, emotional, volitional), and principles of thought (logical, scientific, moral). How we arrange these authorities says something about our moral philosophy: whichever authority we reckon the ultimate and most authoritative is our god.

A righteous moral philosophy makes Yahweh the ultimate authority, for there is none greater (Heb 6:13). Accordingly, *all* our words and deeds must be done according to his authority (Col 3:17), subordinating all other authorities. Whatever is not brought "into captivity to the obedience of Christ" is not neutral but rather "*against* the knowledge of God" (2 Cor 10:5; cf. Matt 12:30). Wishing to avoid the sin of our first parents, therefore, we screen all of our thinking and doing through his authoritative Word (Deut 6:6, 8).

An idolatrous moral philosophy, on the other hand, makes something other than Yahweh the highest authority. We deify anything we make our *ultimate* authority. As ultimate, we believe it is self-authorizing.[116] It requires no proof from any extraneous source; if it needed vindication from something else then it would not be *ultimate*. In the nature of the case, then, we treat it with unquestioning allegiance.

---

113. As per natural theologian, Lee Irons: "My own private opinion is that civil government has the right to recognize same-sex civil unions." "What I Believe."

114. As per Natural Law document, *Catechism of the Catholic Church*, Paragraph 2366.

115. Calvin, *Institutes*, 1.5.12.

116. "'Divine' means having the status of not depending on anything else" (Clouser, *Myth*, 21–22, quoted in Frame, *DCL*, 56).

Moreover, we can exalt anything to an ultimate status—whether personal deities or impersonal principles. And though few have trouble seeing the idolatry of placing Baal, Molech, or Allah before Yahweh, we should see it no less idolatrous when impersonal principles are elevated above him. Additionally, it makes no difference whether these authorities are *always* unlawful or whether they are *in themselves* lawful. Authorities that are always unlawful to follow include personal deities like Baal or Allah, or impersonal principles like "We may lie in order to win arguments."

But to see how authorities lawful in themselves become idolatrous requires more judicious reasoning. Take, for example, the principle to love your family (Titus 2:4)—a good principle in itself. However, when we place this love above Yahweh it becomes sinful (Deut 13:6–10; 1 Sam 2:29; Matt 10:37). Again, seeking help from others is in itself a morally permissible principle (Deut 14:28–29; 2 Sam 10:11; Luke 10:40), but when our hearts trust in man's help more than the Lord's help it becomes immoral (Jer 17:5). Laboring to gain financial profit is another honorable principle (Deut 8:18; Prov 10:4; 13:22; 31:10–31; Eph 4:28), but we idolize money when we place it before the Lord. Commenting on Jesus' warning, "You cannot serve God and mammon" (Matt 6:24; Luke 16:13), Frame says, "Jesus personifies [money], as if it were the name of a god, enhancing the allusion to the first commandment."[117] Our reasoning faculties, moreover, are a gift of God, but when they are used as ultimate authorities they violate God's instructions (Prov 3:5–6), as Calvin wisely understands:

> For [the philosophers] set up reason alone as the ruling principle in man, and think that it alone should be listened to; to it alone, in short, they entrust the conduct of life. But the Christian philosophy bids reason give way to, submit and subject itself to, the Holy Spirit so that the man himself may no longer live but hear Christ living and reigning within him [Gal. 2:20].[118]

We have other gods before Yahweh when we serve anything instead of him, even things lawful in themselves.

Non-Christian philosophers make this especially noticeable. For if God condemns the practice of placing other authorities *above* his, then he all the more condemns practices that have *no* regard for his authority

---

117. Frame, *DCL*, 415n.13.
118. Calvin, *Institutes*, 3.7.1.

whatsoever. When philosophers encourage us to follow their ethic, they usually enjoin on us an ultimate principle. Often this principle can be found in the Bible, but by extracting the principle from biblical authority, they make an idol of it. Kant, for instance, says that a good action stems from a sense of duty; any action looking to beneficial consequences is an immoral action on Kant's terms. Being motivated to behavior out of a sense of duty is quite biblical (Eccl 12:13; Luke 17:10; Rom 13:8). Kant, though, extracts it from God's authority (contrary to 2 Cor 10:5; Col 3:17 et al.), seeing no need of him to make his ultimate principle obligatory. It is self-authorizing, thinks Kant. Egoism's ultimate principle says "Act in your own best interest"—another biblical principle (Deut 6:24; Ps 1:2–3; Matt 6:20; 1 Tim 4:8). Utilitarianism exalts as its highest principle "Act so as to maximize happiness"—again, a Scriptural principle (cp. Deut 6:24 & Deut 28; Ps 2:10–12 & Ps 144:15). Yet, as with Kant, egoism and utilitarianism find no need for Christ in their ethic, and in this they err. These philosophies are no less idolatrous than Islam: "False worship may not involve rites or ceremonies, but it always involves the attribution of aseity [self-authorization] to something."[119] Yet Yahweh requires *exclusive* ultimate allegiance: "You shall have no other gods before Me" (Exod 20:3).[120]

With this background, Natural Law's idolatrous tendency becomes clear. Though it does place nature under God's authority, as when it says "the natural law is in fact given by God and bears its authority from him,"[121] this is not consistently maintained. VanDrunen, for instance, sometimes appeals to common, agreed-upon notions to make a moral case:

> By arguing that particular actions are wrong because they tend to promote killing or stealing (which most people admit are bad things), or by arguing that particular actions are right because they tend to promote life or the protection of property (which most people admit are good things), one may construct natural law arguments that have a certain chance for effectiveness.[122]

---

119. Frame, *DCL*, 57.

120. Deuteronomy 4:2 informs us that by not adding to or subtracting from God's words enables us to keep them ("that you may keep the commandments"), as such deliberate tampering renounces God's authority. Consequently, *no* commandment is obeyed when his authority is renounced.

121. VanDrunen, *Biblical Case*, 7.

122. VanDrunen, "Public Square."

He sometimes makes these common notions the *basis* of moral arguments.[123] He does not attempt to prove them, but simply uses these notions as building blocks to prove grander conclusions. These notions, then, are treated as authoritative in themselves. He obviously is not resting them on God's authority because then they would not be *common*[124] (not to mention he would lose the unbeliever's interest).

However, Van Til rightly says that "the 'common notions' of men are sinful notions."[125] Take, for example, the principle "You shall not murder." What unbelievers and believers understand by this principle differs greatly. Unbelievers assume an impersonal principle that binds all without needing proof; believers, on the other hand, assume an expression of a personal God who alone makes the principle binding. They agree on the principle only formally. Our witness to the God of Scripture "is not presented, however, if we grant that God the Holy Spirit in a general testimony to all men approves of interpretations of this world or of aspects of this world which ignore Him and set Him at naught."[126] Unbelievers, consequently, interpret the principle unrighteously, and VanDrunen does as well when he has *common agreement* with them on these notions.

VanDrunen, though, seems unbothered by this conclusion. He feels justified in ignoring God's authority in such situations:

> And what if . . . my neighbor is not a Christian and does not accept Scripture as a moral authority? . . . I would first of all wish my neighbor to put faith in Christ and believe the Scriptures. But even if she does not, I still would rather she be pro-life in her voting and personal behavior . . . for the sake of a relative social peace and justice.[127]

---

123. For example, arguing against abortion, he writes: "Based upon the social consensus that infanticide is immoral, then, a compelling argument can be made . . ."; and against cloning, he writes: "Beginning with these shared convictions . . ." ("Public Square").

124. He could rescue himself from a sinful moral philosophy by saying that when he and unbelievers "agree" on certain notions, though the unbeliever has no regard for God's authority, he (VanDrunen) still does. By this maneuver, though, he would be equivocating, forfeiting the notions as *common*. Furthermore, in another context he disapproved of such a maneuver, lamenting the "agreements" via ambiguous terminology made by Roman Catholics and Protestants over the doctrine of justification. Having notions common in this way, he says, "ought never happen" (his closing statement in *Law in Modern Times*).

125. Van Til in Bahnsen, *Van Til's Apologetic*, 422.

126. Van Til, *Common Grace*, 145.

127. VanDrunen, "Anxious Kloosterman." As evidenced by this quote, VanDrunen

The unbeliever's internal allegiance, he thinks, is secondary to social peace and justice. VanDrunen makes similar statements in another article:

> If we do attempt to make such [common notion] arguments in a careful and civil way, by God's grace we may make some progress toward moving society in a more just direction.

And:

> As Christians go into the public square and take up their responsibility of interacting with unbelievers for the sake of civil peace and cultural progress, natural law provides an important and helpful resource.[128]

However, we cannot make use of sinful arguments to obtain righteous goals, as Paul forbids us to do evil that good may come (Rom 3:8). God's work must be done by God's ways.[129]

We find, then, an inconsistency concerning the authority of Natural Law. Sometimes God's authority backs the theory, sometimes his authority is implicitly denied. The cause of this inconsistency is not difficult to discern. Appealing to God's authority has its advantages: it avoids the naturalistic fallacy, a fallacy so common and fearlessly wielded by secular Natural Law ethicists; it avoids idolatry, that is, advocating an authority independent from God's authority; and it creates a sympathetic hearing from theists who are predisposed to God's authority. However, it does have a major disadvantage: it loses its common appeal—which is what attracts some theologians to Natural Law—since unbelievers do

---

sometimes misses the point of objections to his position. Everybody "would rather she be pro-life in her voting and personal behavior," but this is irrelevant to the *authority* for her decisions. Likewise in answering the charge that his position utilizes pagan notions, he answers that we all must "live lives *in common* with unbelievers in a range of cultural activities"—again confusing cooperation in cultural activities with the internal allegiance for those activities. In this same article, VanDrunen confuses civil right with moral right: "Do I tell [my unbelieving neighbor] that if she does not submit to the Scriptures then she has no right to participate in the political process?"

128. VanDrunen, "Public Square."

129. Not to mention that the good goals VanDrunen seeks (i.e., social peace and justice) come only by obedience, not sin (Deut 28; 2 Chr 15:1-6; Prov 14:34; Jer 18:7-11). Calvin likewise held that God's Word best suits God's world, recognizing the connection between profitability and ethics: "all welfare proceeds from the hand of God, and that there is no way to prosper except by giving ourselves over to Him, and to His service" (*Covenant Enforced*, 96). The Christianization of the nations comes by knowing and dutifully applying the King's Word.

not accept God's authority.[130] Conversely, making Natural Law rest on an authority independent from God's authority has an advantage as well: it creates a sympathetic hearing from unbelievers. Although the disadvantages are great: without God's authority, it commits the naturalistic fallacy; it makes Natural Law idolatrous; and it loses (or at least should lose) its Christian support.

As a result, natural theologians run from pillar to post trying to vindicate Natural Law: We need an agreed-upon standard to rule society, they say. But what gives this standard binding authority? God, they say. Can we then appeal to his Word since we appeal to his authority? No, because we need an agreed-upon standard. What gives the standard authority? God. Can we use his Word since we use his authority? No, we need agreed-upon standards. And on and on it goes.[131]

Frame appropriately laments, "Too often, in ethical debate, Christians sound too much like unbelievers. . . . I believe they almost inevitably give this false impression when they are reasoning according to natural law alone."[132] Unbelievers' interpretations of nature are the last thing with which we ought to seek common agreement, for "the world by its wisdom knows not God and not knowing God it knows not the world."[133] As Christ forcefully declares that whatever is not built on his words will crumble (Matt 7:24–27), Natural Law is no exception. We have seen it commit three major flaws: (a) Confining biblical instruction to believers, it contradicts the Bible's own claims of itself as universally

---

130. Additionally, when God's authority backs the theory, it is no longer a Natural Law but rather a *Super*-Natural Law.

131. What is more, since Christ now mediates *all* of the Father's authority (Matt 28:18; John 5:22, 27; 1 Cor 15:27), we can also fault VanDrunen for abstracting civil morality from Christ's kingdom. For as Christ is King of all earthly rulers (Rev 17:14; 19:16), they *in their official capacity* must submit to him (Ps 2:10–12). And though only believers will recognize his rule (John 3:3, 5), the obligation to recognize it nonetheless rests upon all. He has been enthroned over all the earth, not just the church (Dan 7:13–14; Matt 13:38; 28:18–20; Eph 1:20–23), and it is the whole world, not just the church, currently being redeemed (Acts 3:21; 1 Cor 15:24–27; Col 1:19–20). As a result, every moral law of God, including those applicable to the civil realm, points to faith in Christ as a prerequisite to obeying it (Rom 10:4). Accordingly, Paul had no scruples against interchanging "Christ" with Mosaic "commandment" (cp. Rom 10:6–7 and Deut 30:12–13). Therefore, any Christ-*less* moral philosophy is sin*ful*.

132. Frame, "Natural Revelation." For example, Natural theologians sound much like humanist professor, Paul Kurtz, who exhorts us to follow the "common moral decencies" (*Living Without Religion*, 41).

133. Van Til in Bahnsen, *Van Til's Apologetic*, 712.

binding (Rom 3:19); (b) separating nature from Scripture's gospel and Scripture's interpretations of nature, it leads to a corrupt moral philosophy; and worst of all, (c) equivocating on its authority, it sometimes bases itself on something other than God's authority, making an idol out of nature—worshiping the creation rather than the Creator (Rom 1:25). Furthermore, we should not advocate a philosophy that keeps God's Word from people—knowing that when God withholds his Word, leaving people to natural revelation alone, he intends to leave them in their sins (Acts 14:16; 17:30). We should rather advocate a philosophy that conveys the words bringing happiness to a community (Prov 29:18). Christians should always, like brave young David, encounter the world "in the name of the LORD of hosts" (1 Sam 17:45). We must not hesitate between two philosophies, but must follow the exhortation of Elijah: "if the LORD is God, follow Him" (1 Kgs 18:21). Dear Christian, always avoid doctrines that encourage you to leave your Bible aside; but rather, in every matter "Let the *word* of Christ dwell in you richly" (Col 3:16).

BENEFITS OF THIS BOOK

So to a civilization content, even eager, to live by bread alone, the voice of God must be proclaimed, indeed, his *every* proceeding word. Christians must resist tendencies to truncate or supplant heavenly instruction; as Calvin warns, "God declares that all are apostates who do not confine themselves to the simplicity of the Law."[134]

Weak ethical teaching not only betrays our Lord but also handicaps our behavior. On the one hand, the authoritative *generalities* of Antinomianism tend to immobilize us. Not that there is anything wrong with divine general directions; whatever the Lord speaks to us ought to inspire our highest honors. Such was the human situation before Mosaic revelation. "When God reveals his will at a general level, we should try to implement the specifics by our sanctified human wisdom."[135] However, the more human reasoning involved the more susceptibility to error. What a blessing it is, therefore, when God himself reasons out from the generalities. "When he reveals his will more specifically, we should be grateful for that additional guidance."[136] It has been the practice of modern American Christendom, though, in cutting off Mosaic

---

134. Calvin, *Commentaries*, Deut 11:16.
135. Frame, *DCL*, 480.
136. Frame, *DCL*, 480.

details, to offer the world only generalities. As a result, few today look to Christians for answers to economic, parental, educational, social, or political problems. Since ambiguities and generalities offer little solace to those in ethical entanglements, Christianity is too often tossed into the trash heap of irrelevancy.

When the thought arises, for example, of a burglar breaking into your home, you want more instructions than "protect your family." Does this protection involve lethal force? What if it is clear that the burglar only wants your jewelry and intends no bodily harm? One of the bullet-point entries in this book summarizing Calvin's comments on Exodus 22:1–4 is particularly helpful:

> The exception concerning the thief in the night (vv. 2–3a) is parenthetical to the overall passage. A man who kills a thief in the night is free from punishment because he could not see the behavior of the thief and because it is likely that a thief in the night will resort to violence since in the night he may only enter a house by violent damage. But if the thief is discovered in the day, when sunlight exposes the criminal, the killing is accounted murder and penalized by execution, for killing is too severe for theft.

What should a father do whose daughter has been seduced by a man? The advice "flee sexual immorality" is much too general (and too late!). Inquiring fathers may refer to Calvin's comments on Exodus 22:16–17, summarized in this book as follows:

- Here God shows his care for young females, who, being deceived by a man, loses her virginity, with the seducer refusing to covenant with her.
- To prevent her despairing abandonment to prostitution (since she has lost her virginity), God requires the man to marry her. The man must also give her a dowry from his own property, lest if he should cast her off, she should not go away penniless.
- The father, however, can refuse her suitor while yet keeping the dowry.

Not only do these details instruct a society on how to deter carefree seductions and abandonments, but they also mobilize a concerned father to bring about the best results for his daughter from a potentially ruinous situation.

We could ask more about other matters that confront us everyday: What should be the criteria of electing civil rulers? Are candidates' religious convictions relevant? What should be our attitude toward policies that debase our money? Those who have retired, who have saved money for this stage in their life, find their money worth less through no fault of their own. Are they justified for resenting such economic policies? And what of civil rulers, whose duty it is to protect the innocent and deter crime? The general dictum, "Rulers should be just," offers little help to them. How do they deter dog attacks, car theft, rape, or false accusations? What should they do, if anything, with criminals who seek asylum in churches? What should be done to those who carelessly start a fire that destroys another's property? Is *any* penalty permissible to captured terrorists? Those charged with protecting citizens want more direction than "the punishment must fit the crime." Will not he deserve punishment who limits counsel to such vagueness!

Generalities give the parent, the voter, the retired, and the magistrate little direction for the issues of life, and therefore little propulsion for action. Bahnsen said it well: "Even today, when God's people get embroiled in moral dilemmas, they desire more inspired law (guidance), not less. It is surely no blessing to be left only with broad generalities: e.g., see how many people are blessed and happy by trying to play a basketball game under the single rule of 'Play fair'!"[137] God indeed gave through Moses many detailed instructions "for our good" (Deut 6:24; cf. 10:13).[138]

On the other hand, the *unauthoritative* specifics of Natural Law conduces uncertainty. Just any philosophy supplying specifics will not

---

137. Bahnsen, *Five Views*, 65.

138. Once Antinomians recognize the lack of specifics in their moral system, they have different reactions. One reaction is agnosticism toward specifics: "It is more difficult to determine whether the law of Christ includes specific teachings and principles" (Moo, *Five Views*, 369). Another is contentment with agnosticism: "We may, however, have to live with a situation in which we are not given such clear guidance about the form and function of government" (Moo, *Five Views*, 173). Fear of specifics is another reaction: "Having recognized the place within 'the law of Christ' of specific commandments, however, I want to insist that they must not be given too much prominence" (Moo, *Five Views*, 370). So though specifics have a place, whatever that might be, this writer warns against paying too much attention to them! A fourth reaction is to glory in generalizations: "This 'law [of Christ]' is not a set of rules but a set of principles" (Moo, *Five Views*, 357). Morey so glories in his generalized ethic that he says it is a sign of a mature church to need particulars no longer. "But now," he says, "since the coming of Christ, the people of God have 'come of age' and no longer need to be told how to do such things as if they were still children" (*Relate*, 44). Yet even these men know that generalizations will not go far. So, lastly, they attempt strategies to arrive at particulars: "We must take the biblical directives and use the sanctified wisdom and common sense described in Proverbs to apply them to all of life" (Morey, *Relate*, 46); and: "The only alternative we have, and one that many thoughtful Christians follow, is to seek divine wisdom in translating the moral teaching of Scripture into the civil realm" (Moo, *Five Views*, 173). Has not Omniscience already done this in the Mosaic Law?

do. For even when its conclusions are true (e.g., that abortions are immoral), our consciences have little peace until we know God approves. Calvin put it this way, "men's consciences shall by no other means be quiet, that they safely do that which they do, than when being taught by the Word of God, they determine that they do nothing without his commandment and conduct."[139] To God we admit: "Great peace have those who love Your law" (Ps 119:165).

In conclusion, this book benefits the reader by supplying ethical *specifics*, mobilizing us from idleness caused by ignorance; and by supplying the *Lord's* specifics, driving away uncertainty and giving peace to our troubled souls. A third benefit, as said previously, is it provides an *expedited ethics education*. For since God's Law covers the *whole* of righteous ethics, and since the Mosaic Law is the most detailed and concentrated formulation of God's Law, and since Calvin (one of the best theologians God has ever given his church) has beneficially organized the Mosaic Law, this summary of Calvin gives moral instructions on the *whole* of our duty. Indeed, "it is an inestimable benefit when God shows us His will,"[140] but as God's will is meaty, this book, in a way, "cuts up the meat" for Christ's little ones.

The Reformed faith is renowned for its moral concerns: "From [Calvin's] time to the present Calvinism has meant a peculiar seriousness about Christianity and its ethical implications."[141] As loyal subjects of the King, we wish to see his rule duly recognized over all the earth. But let us not entertain the foolish thought that this can come without knowledge of God's Law. As the King informs us, his kingdom will not come apart from his will being done on earth as it is in heaven (Matt 6:10). "So then do not be foolish," dear reader, but read on to "understand what the will of the Lord is" (Eph 5:17, NASB). A confused and broken world awaits divine direction.

GOD'S WILL BE DONE

---

139. Calvin, *Commentary*, Acts 10:20.
140. Calvin, *Covenant Enforced*, 85.
141. *Encyclopedia Britannica*, s.v. "Calvin and Calvinism," 15:454.

Preface to the Decalogue

*I am the LORD your God, who brought you
out of the land of Egypt, out of the house of bondage.*

Purposes: *To dignify the Law and to prepare our minds for its reception.*

Exod 20:1–2

And God spoke all these words, saying: ² "I am the Lord your God, who brought you out of the land of Egypt, out of the house of bondage."

Deut 5:1–6

And Moses called all Israel, and said to them: "Hear, O Israel, the statutes and judgments which I speak in your hearing today, that you may learn them and be careful to observe them. ²The Lord our God made a covenant with us in Horeb. ³The Lord did not make this covenant with our fathers, but with us, those who are here today, all of us who are alive. ⁴The Lord talked with you face to face on the mountain from the midst of the fire. ⁵I stood between the Lord and you at that time, to declare to you the word of the Lord; for you were afraid because of the fire, and you did not go up the mountain. He said: ⁶'I am the Lord your God who brought you out of the land of Egypt, out of the house of bondage.'"

Deut 4:20

But the Lord has taken you and brought you out of the iron furnace, out of Egypt, to be His people, an inheritance, as you are this day.

- God comes forth before the people in his dignity to devote them to himself, to claim the authority he deserves, and to prepare their minds for obedience.
- God declares himself as Jehovah, and that Israel is his peculiar people by virtue of their special redemption. This is calculated to attract them gently to his Law that it may be to them more precious than gold and silver and sweeter than honey (Ps 119:72, 103).
- God reminds them of their former servile condition, likening Egypt to a house of bondage and an iron furnace.

- Moses reminds the people that God had covenanted with them, wherefore they should eagerly embrace the Law, and that this special blessing was more than their fathers had received who God left to die in Egypt.

Lev 19:36–37

I am the Lord your God, who brought you out of the land of Egypt. ³⁷Therefore you shall observe all My statutes and all My judgments, and perform them: I am the Lord.

Lev 20:8

And you shall keep My statutes, and perform them: I am the Lord who sanctifies you.

Lev 22:31–33

Therefore you shall keep My commandments, and perform them: I am the Lord. ³²You shall not profane My holy name, but I will be hallowed among the children of Israel. I am the Lord who sanctifies you, ³³who brought you out of the land of Egypt, to be your God: I am the Lord.

Deut 4:1–2

Now, O Israel, listen to the statutes and the judgments which I teach you to observe, that you may live, and go in and possess the land which the Lord God of your fathers is giving you. ²You shall not add to the word which I command you, nor take from it, that you may keep the commandments of the Lord your God which I command you.

Deut 5:32–33

Therefore you shall be careful to do as the Lord your God has commanded you; you shall not turn aside to the right hand or to the left. ³³You shall walk in all the ways which the Lord your God has commanded you, that you may live and that it may be well with you, and that you may prolong your days in the land which you shall possess.

Deut 13:18

. . . because you have listened to the voice of the Lord your God, to keep all His commandments which I command you today, to do what is right in the eyes of the Lord your God.

- Exhorting his people to obedience, God again declares his authority and redemption. This redemption is both past ("who brought you out of the land of Egypt") and present/future ("who sanctifies you").

- As God hallows his people, he requires them likewise to hallow his name by their obedience to his Law.
- God requires of his people a teachable attitude, whereby they might attentively seek direction from his Law.
- Only those who confine themselves to the Law, adding or subtracting nothing from its teaching, are true disciples of it. And to dispose to obedience, a promise of a long and prosperous life is subjoined to this command.

DEUT 4:5-14

Surely I have taught you statutes and judgments, just as the LORD my God commanded me, that you should act according to them in the land which you go to possess. ⁶Therefore be careful to observe them; for this is your wisdom and your understanding in the sight of the peoples who will hear all these statutes, and say, "Surely this great nation is a wise and understanding people." ⁷For what great nation is there that has God so near to it, as the LORD our God is to us, for whatever reason we may call upon Him? ⁸And what great nation is there that has such statutes and righteous judgments as are in all this law which I set before you this day? ⁹Only take heed to yourself, and diligently keep yourself, lest you forget the things your eyes have seen, and lest they depart from your heart all the days of your life. And teach them to your children and your grandchildren, ¹⁰especially concerning the day you stood before the LORD your God in Horeb, when the LORD said to me, "Gather the people to Me, and I will let them hear My words, that they may learn to fear Me all the days they live on the earth, and that they may teach their children." ¹¹Then you came near and stood at the foot of the mountain, and the mountain burned with fire to the midst of heaven, with darkness, cloud, and thick darkness. ¹²And the LORD spoke to you out of the midst of the fire. You heard the sound of the words, but saw no form; you only heard a voice. ¹³So He declared to you His covenant which He commanded you to perform, the Ten Commandments; and He wrote them on two tablets of stone. ¹⁴And the LORD commanded me at that time to teach you statutes and judgments, that you might observe them in the land which you cross over to possess.

- God teaches the people that nothing is more beneficial than obedience to his Law.

- A stage had been erected whereby the entire world would marvel and envy Israel if they should implement and keep his statutes.

- God warns against slothfulness and forgetting what great things he has done before their eyes. He exhorts his people to remember his wonders and to pass down this knowledge to posterity.

DEUT 4:32–40

For ask now concerning the days that are past, which were before you, since the day that God created man on the earth, and ask from one end of heaven to the other, whether any great thing like this has happened, or anything like it has been heard. [33]Did any people ever hear the voice of God speaking out of the midst of the fire, as you have heard, and live? [34]Or did God ever try to go and take for Himself a nation from the midst of another nation, by trials, by signs, by wonders, by war, by a mighty hand and an outstretched arm, and by great terrors, according to all that the LORD your God did for you in Egypt before your eyes? [35]To you it was shown, that you might know that the LORD Himself is God; there is none other besides Him. [36]Out of heaven He let you hear His voice, that He might instruct you; on earth He showed you His great fire, and you heard His words out of the midst of the fire. [37]And because He loved your fathers, therefore He chose their descendants after them; and He brought you out of Egypt with His Presence, with His mighty power, [38]driving out from before you nations greater and mightier than you, to bring you in, to give you their land as an inheritance, as it is this day. [39]Therefore know this day, and consider it in your heart, that the LORD Himself is God in heaven above and on the earth beneath; there is no other. [40]You shall therefore keep His statutes and His commandments which I command you today, that it may go well with you and with your children after you, and that you may prolong your days in the land which the LORD your God is giving you for all time.

- Greater sanctions of the Law are given on account of the many miracles done for Israel, noting that nothing like these had been done since creation. And as Israel knew these miracles, and that this Law was given by him, disobedience would be inexcusable.

- Whatever good God had bestowed on Israel was gracious, being motivated out of love for the patriarchs and their posterity.

Deut 7:6–8

For you are a holy people to the Lord *your God; the* Lord *your God has chosen you to be a people for Himself, a special treasure above all the peoples on the face of the earth.* ⁷*The* Lord *did not set His love on you nor choose you because you were more in number than any other people, for you were the least of all peoples;* ⁸*but because the* Lord *loves you, and because He would keep the oath which He swore to your fathers, the* Lord *has brought you out with a mighty hand, and redeemed you from the house of bondage, from the hand of Pharaoh king of Egypt.*

Deut 10:14–17

Indeed heaven and the highest heavens belong to the Lord *your God, also the earth with all that is in it.* ¹⁵*The* Lord *delighted only in your fathers, to love them; and He chose their descendants after them, you above all peoples, as it is this day.* ¹⁶*Therefore circumcise the foreskin of your heart, and be stiff-necked no longer.* ¹⁷*For the* Lord *your God is God of gods and Lord of lords, the great God, mighty and awesome, who shows no partiality nor takes a bribe.*

- God declares that the purpose of Israel's election was to acquire unto himself a holy people, pure from all pollutions (see 1 Thess 4:7; 1 Pet 2:9).
- The passing over of all other nations expresses the graciousness of Israel's call, and Moses mentions it to motivate faithful submission to their deliverer.
- The Jews are obliged to circumcise their hearts, as men are not naturally disposed to heed God. Self-renunciation and a subduing of carnal affections are required for right living.

Deut 27:9–10

Then Moses and the priests, the Levites, spoke to all Israel, saying, "Take heed and listen, O Israel: This day you have become the people of the Lord *your God.* ¹⁰*Therefore you shall obey the voice of the* Lord *your God, and observe His commandments and His statutes which I command you today."*

- God again lays the Israelites under obligation to his statutes on the basis of his adoption.

Deut 26:16–19

This day the Lord your God commands you to observe these statutes and judgments; therefore you shall be careful to observe them with all your heart and with all your soul. ¹⁷Today you have proclaimed the Lord to be your God, and that you will walk in His ways and keep His statutes, His commandments, and His judgments, and that you will obey His voice. ¹⁸Also today the Lord has proclaimed you to be His special people, just as He promised you, that you should keep all His commandments, ¹⁹and that He will set you high above all nations which He has made, in praise, in name, and in honor, and that you may be a holy people to the Lord your God, just as He has spoken.

- As people easily grow indifferent to righteousness, God again exhorts earnest obedience.
- God requires us to keep his Law with all our heart and soul, that is, with serious and sincere apprehension and without duplicity.
- Obedience would, by God's promised blessing, excel Israel far above all nations.

Deut 6:20–25

When your son asks you in time to come, saying, "What is the meaning of the testimonies, the statutes, and the judgments which the Lord our God has commanded you?" ²¹then you shall say to your son: "We were slaves of Pharaoh in Egypt, and the Lord brought us out of Egypt with a mighty hand; ²²and the Lord showed signs and wonders before our eyes, great and severe, against Egypt, Pharaoh, and all his household. ²³Then He brought us out from there, that He might bring us in, to give us the land of which He swore to our fathers. ²⁴And the Lord commanded us to observe all these statutes, to fear the Lord our God, for our good always, that He might preserve us alive, as it is this day. ²⁵Then it will be righteousness for us, if we are careful to observe all these commandments before the Lord our God, as He has commanded us."

- The people should testify their gratitude for their redemption by obeying his Law and by teaching posterity the religion handed to them.
- Moses sums up the Law by "to fear the Lord." Performance of commandments is hardly sufficient without inner fear and

worship of God. Lives are not duly ordered if they only exercise equity towards others while depriving God of his right.

- Law obedience is commended not only out of care for God's own rights, but also for our own profitableness, being "for our good always."

Num 15:37–41

Again the Lord spoke to Moses, saying, ³⁸"Speak to the children of Israel: Tell them to make tassels on the corners of their garments throughout their generations, and to put a blue thread in the tassels of the corners. ³⁹And you shall have the tassel, that you may look upon it and remember all the commandments of the Lord and do them, and that you may not follow the harlotry to which your own heart and your own eyes are inclined, ⁴⁰and that you may remember and do all My commandments, and be holy for your God. ⁴¹I am the Lord your God, who brought you out of the land of Egypt, to be your God: I am the Lord your God."

Deut 6:6–9

And these words which I command you today shall be in your heart. ⁷You shall teach them diligently to your children, and shall talk of them when you sit in your house, when you walk by the way, when you lie down, and when you rise up. ⁸You shall bind them as a sign on your hand, and they shall be as frontlets between your eyes. ⁹You shall write them on the doorposts of your house and on your gates.

Deut 11:18–20

Therefore you shall lay up these words of mine in your heart and in your soul, and bind them as a sign on your hand, and they shall be as frontlets between your eyes. ¹⁹You shall teach them to your children, speaking of them when you sit in your house, when you walk by the way, when you lie down, and when you rise up. ²⁰And you shall write them on the doorposts of your house and on your gates, . . .

Exod 23:13

And in all that I have said to you, be circumspect and make no mention of the name of other gods, nor let it be heard from your mouth.

- As people are lazy and forgetful, God made use of material aids (viz., fringes on garments, bracelets, frontlets) to stir up remembrance of the Law and to cultivate piety.

- People "follow harlotry" whenever they are governed by their own counsels, rather than by his Law.
- Moses urges believers to teach each other the Lord's commandments throughout the whole day and in all of their activities (cf. Ps 1:2).

Deut 27:1–4, 8

Now Moses, with the elders of Israel, commanded the people, saying: "Keep all the commandments which I command you today. ²And it shall be, on the day when you cross over the Jordan to the land which the Lord your God is giving you, that you shall set up for yourselves large stones, and whitewash them with lime. ³You shall write on them all the words of this law, when you have crossed over, that you may enter the land which the Lord your God is giving you, 'a land flowing with milk and honey,' just as the Lord God of your fathers promised you. ⁴Therefore it shall be, when you have crossed over the Jordan, that on Mount Ebal you shall set up these stones, which I command you today, and you shall whitewash them with lime. . . . ⁸And you shall write very plainly on the stones all the words of this law."

- God required the erection of a monument at the entrance of the Land. On it should be written his laws that whoever entered might know that they entered the sanctuary of heavenly doctrine and thereby might worship God purely.

Deut 31:10–13

And Moses commanded them, saying: "At the end of every seven years, at the appointed time in the year of release, at the Feast of Tabernacles, ¹¹when all Israel comes to appear before the Lord your God in the place which He chooses, you shall read this law before all Israel in their hearing. ¹²Gather the people together, men and women and little ones, and the stranger who is within your gates, that they may hear and that they may learn to fear the Lord your God and carefully observe all the words of this law, ¹³and that their children, who have not known it, may hear and learn to fear the Lord your God as long as you live in the land which you cross the Jordan to possess."

- The Law was to be recited every seventh year in the place where God would choose, that its knowledge may never depart. This was to be done by the Levites to the assembled Israelites during the Feast of Tabernacles.

Deut 6:10–12

So it shall be, when the Lord your God brings you into the land of which He swore to your fathers, to Abraham, Isaac, and Jacob, to give you large and beautiful cities which you did not build, ¹¹houses full of all good things, which you did not fill, hewn-out wells which you did not dig, vineyards and olive trees which you did not plant—when you have eaten and are full— ¹²then beware, lest you forget the Lord who brought you out of the land of Egypt, from the house of bondage.

- Since wealth and prosperity often blind people's minds, God anticipates this by warning against forgetting him when they come to occupy a land with many blessings (see Deut 32:15).

Deut 9:1–6

Hear, O Israel: You are to cross over the Jordan today, and go in to dispossess nations greater and mightier than yourself, cities great and fortified up to heaven, ²a people great and tall, the descendants of the Anakim, whom you know, and of whom you heard it said, "Who can stand before the descendants of Anak?" ³Therefore understand today that the Lord your God is He who goes over before you as a consuming fire. He will destroy them and bring them down before you; so you shall drive them out and destroy them quickly, as the Lord has said to you. ⁴Do not think in your heart, after the Lord your God has cast them out before you, saying, "Because of my righteousness the Lord has brought me in to possess this land"; but it is because of the wickedness of these nations that the Lord is driving them out from before you. ⁵It is not because of your righteousness or the uprightness of your heart that you go in to possess their land, but because of the wickedness of these nations that the Lord your God drives them out from before you, and that He may fulfill the word which the Lord swore to your fathers, to Abraham, Isaac, and Jacob. ⁶Therefore understand that the Lord your God is not giving you this good land to possess because of your righteousness, for you are a stiff-necked people.

- God, by his signal bounty, and through no merit of the people, made Israel to inherit Canaan. This bounty flowed from the covenant made with the patriarchs, from Israel's adoption into it, and from the wickedness of the Canaanites. Israel in turn should persevere in faithful observation of this covenant.

- God warns them against attributing victories and possession of the Land to their own valor, thereby defrauding him of glory.

And Moses is not content with the admission that God helped, but requires full acknowledgment of God's works and that Israel deserved nothing of the kind. If this is the case with regard to earthly Canaan, how much more arrogant is it to claim credit for a heavenly inheritance!

- God exalts his glory by noting Israel's soon to be victories over fortified nations and peoples mightier and bigger than they.

DEUT 10:21–22

He is your praise, and He is your God, who has done for you these great and awesome things which your eyes have seen. ²²Your fathers went down to Egypt with seventy persons, and now the LORD your God has made you as the stars of heaven in multitude.

DEUT 11:1–7

Therefore you shall love the LORD your God, and keep His charge, His statutes, His judgments, and His commandments always. ²Know today that I do not speak with your children, who have not known and who have not seen the chastening of the LORD your God, His greatness and His mighty hand and His outstretched arm— ³His signs and His acts which He did in the midst of Egypt, to Pharaoh king of Egypt, and to all his land; ⁴what He did to the army of Egypt, to their horses and their chariots: how He made the waters of the Red Sea overflow them as they pursued you, and how the LORD has destroyed them to this day; ⁵what He did for you in the wilderness until you came to this place; ⁶and what He did to Dathan and Abiram the sons of Eliab, the son of Reuben: how the earth opened its mouth and swallowed them up, their households, their tents, and all the substance that was in their possession, in the midst of all Israel— ⁷but your eyes have seen every great act of the LORD which He did.

- Moses declares God to be the people's honor and ornament ("your praise"). And proving that the Lord is Israel's God, Moses notes many of his miracles on their behalf, and calls forth their own eyes as witnesses that they might be more inexcusable for rejecting him.
- The Law is called God's "charge" (i.e., a guard) because it fences in our life with rails lest we be exposed to errors on the right or left.

DEUT 8:1–6

Every commandment which I command you today you must be careful to observe, that you may live and multiply, and go in and possess the land of which the LORD swore to your fathers. ²And you shall remember that the LORD your God led you all the way these forty years in the wilderness, to humble you and test you, to know what was in your heart, whether you would keep His commandments or not. ³So He humbled you, allowed you to hunger, and fed you with manna which you did not know nor did your fathers know, that He might make you know that man shall not live by bread alone; but man lives by every word that proceeds from the mouth of the LORD. ⁴Your garments did not wear out on you, nor did your foot swell these forty years. ⁵You should know in your heart that as a man chastens his son, so the LORD your God chastens you. ⁶Therefore you shall keep the commandments of the LORD your God, to walk in His ways and to fear Him.

DEUT 11:8–9

Therefore you shall keep every commandment which I command you today, that you may be strong, and go in and possess the land which you cross over to possess, ⁹and that you may prolong your days in the land which the LORD swore to give your fathers, to them and their descendants, "a land flowing with milk and honey."

- God indicates that he had proved them for forty years in the desert, humbling them with afflictions to know what was in their heart. By being made to suffer hunger and to have their garments remain whole after forty years of use they learned that they lived by God's secret power. By these God shows us not to tie our minds to the elements as if they supplied our needs, but to look higher, indeed, to what proceeds from his mouth.

DEUT 29:2–9

Now Moses called all Israel and said to them: "You have seen all that the LORD did before your eyes in the land of Egypt, to Pharaoh and to all his servants and to all his land— ³the great trials which your eyes have seen, the signs, and those great wonders. ⁴Yet the LORD has not given you a heart to perceive and eyes to see and ears to hear, to this very day. ⁵And I have led you forty years in the wilderness. Your clothes have not worn out on you, and your sandals have not worn out on your feet. ⁶You have not eaten bread, nor have you drunk wine or similar drink, that you may know that I am the Lord *your God.* ⁷*And when you came to this place, Sihon king of Heshbon and Og king of Bashan came out against us to battle, and we conquered them.* ⁸*We took their land and gave it as an inheritance to the Reubenites, to the Gadites, and to half the tribe of Manasseh.* ⁹*Therefore keep the words of this covenant, and do them, that you may prosper in all that you do."*

- Moses reproves the Jews for not properly acknowledging the miracles that God had done in their sight. He gives as the ultimate reason for this failure God's withholding of his grace, which is necessary to read events rightly.
- Moses again reminds the church that God had manifested his miracles that they might submit themselves to his rule.
- The 2½ tribes that had already taken possession of the land east of the Jordan were held up as a mirror, assuring that the rest of the Promised Land awaited them also.
- Another promise of prosperity is held out to them if they keep the Law.

Deut 8:7–10

For the Lord *your God is bringing you into a good land, a land of brooks of water, of fountains and springs, that flow out of valleys and hills;* ⁸*a land of wheat and barley, of vines and fig trees and pomegranates, a land of olive oil and honey;* ⁹*a land in which you will eat bread without scarcity, in which you will lack nothing; a land whose stones are iron and out of whose hills you can dig copper.* ¹⁰*When you have eaten and are full, then you shall bless the* Lord *your God for the good land which He has given you.*

Deut 11:10–12

For the land which you go to possess is not like the land of Egypt from which you have come, where you sowed your seed and watered it by foot, as a vegetable garden; ¹¹*but the land which you cross over to possess is a land of hills and valleys, which drinks water from the rain of heaven,* ¹²*a land for which the* Lord *your God cares; the eyes of the* Lord *your God are always on it, from the beginning of the year to the very end of the year.*

Deut 6:1–3, 17–19

Now this is the commandment, and these are the statutes and judgments which the Lord your God has commanded to teach you, that you may observe them in the land which you are crossing over to possess, ²that you may fear the Lord your God, to keep all His statutes and His commandments which I command you, you and your son and your grandson, all the days of your life, and that your days may be prolonged. ³Therefore hear, O Israel, and be careful to observe it, that it may be well with you, and that you may multiply greatly as the Lord God of your fathers has promised you— "a land flowing with milk and honey." . . . ¹⁷You shall diligently keep the commandments of the Lord your God, His testimonies, and His statutes which He has commanded you. ¹⁸And you shall do what is right and good in the sight of the Lord, that it may be well with you, and that you may go in and possess the good land of which the Lord swore to your fathers, ¹⁹to cast out all your enemies from before you, as the Lord has spoken.

- God further entices the people to obedience by recounting the many blessings of the land (e.g., full of minerals and water), requiring gratitude from them.

Deut 8:11–18

Beware that you do not forget the Lord your God by not keeping His commandments, His judgments, and His statutes which I command you today, ¹²lest—when you have eaten and are full, and have built beautiful houses and dwell in them; ¹³and when your herds and your flocks multiply, and your silver and your gold are multiplied, and all that you have is multiplied; ¹⁴when your heart is lifted up, and you forget the Lord your God who brought you out of the land of Egypt, from the house of bondage; ¹⁵who led you through that great and terrible wilderness, in which were fiery serpents and scorpions and thirsty land where there was no water; who brought water for you out of the flinty rock; ¹⁶who fed you in the wilderness with manna, which your fathers did not know, that He might humble you and that He might test you, to do you good in the end—¹⁷then you say in your heart, "My power and the might of my hand have gained me this wealth." ¹⁸And you shall remember the Lord your God, for it is He who gives you power to get wealth, that He may establish His covenant which He swore to your fathers, as it is this day.

- God again warns the people of allowing prosperity to elicit ingratitude once entering the Land, thereby causing forgetfulness of God and his covenant. Exhortations to remember God's graces and his Law are accordingly adjoined (cf. 1 Tim 6:17).
- Moses sought to tame their arrogance by recalling their lowly slave condition from which God rescued them, and from his protecting and sustaining them in the wilderness.
- Sometimes God deprives us of necessities that our senses may awaken to acknowledge his aid.
- This is the principal ground of pride: to assume that we have gained by our own exertions, industry, or foresight what God has given us of his own pleasure.

Exod 23:20–23, 25–31

Behold, I send an Angel before you to keep you in the way and to bring you into the place which I have prepared. [21]Beware of Him and obey His voice; do not provoke Him, for He will not pardon your transgressions; for My name is in Him. [22]But if you indeed obey His voice and do all that I speak, then I will be an enemy to your enemies and an adversary to your adversaries. [23]For My Angel will go before you and bring you in to the Amorites and the Hittites and the Perizzites and the Canaanites and the Hivites and the Jebusites; and I will cut them off. . . . [25]So you shall serve the LORD your God, and He will bless your bread and your water. And I will take sickness away from the midst of you. [26]No one shall suffer miscarriage or be barren in your land; I will fulfill the number of your days. [27]I will send My fear before you, I will cause confusion among all the people to whom you come, and will make all your enemies turn their backs to you. [28]And I will send hornets before you, which shall drive out the Hivite, the Canaanite, and the Hittite from before you. [29]I will not drive them out from before you in one year, lest the land become desolate and the beasts of the field become too numerous for you. [30]Little by little I will drive them out from before you, until you have increased, and you inherit the land. [31]And I will set your bounds from the Red Sea to the sea, Philistia, and from the desert to the River. For I will deliver the inhabitants of the land into your hand, and you shall drive them out before you.

- Here is another reminder to Israel that their well-being is connected with their keeping of the Law and that by neglecting it they would sorely suffer.
- God gives a token of his fatherly love by telling them that he would lead them by the hand of an Angel.
- The Angel was Christ (1 Cor 10:9), who has always been the head of the church.
- Lest the Jews become discouraged by a slow and progressive driving out of the enemy, God explains that this was to their advantage, so that the animals not be more troublesome to them than the enemies themselves.
- By naming again the boundaries of the Promised Land, God refers to the covenant once made with their fathers in order to evoke from them a proper response to his unmerited favor.

DEUT 29:29

The secret things belong to the LORD our God, but those things which are revealed belong to us and to our children forever, that we may do all the words of this law.

DEUT 30:11–14

For this commandment which I command you today is not too mysterious for you, nor is it far off. ^{12}It is not in heaven, that you should say, "Who will ascend into heaven for us and bring it to us, that we may hear it and do it?" ^{13}Nor is it beyond the sea, that you should say, "Who will go over the sea for us and bring it to us, that we may hear it and do it?" ^{14}But the word is very near you, in your mouth and in your heart, that you may do it.

- God condemns audacity and excessive curiosity, but commends a zealous seeking of instruction by embracing the doctrine of the Law that he has declared to us.
- This revealed instruction is neglected, turned from in disgust, or treated as obscure by men. Moses, however, bids us to follow it because it is easy and clear.
- Moses is not teaching that keeping the Law is in their power, but rather enjoins the people to be diligent students of the Law, and that they will easily understand it.

- As Paul accommodates this passage to the Gospel (Rom 10:8), he notes that merely comprehending the Law in the mind would profit nothing unless a disposition to obey, which is supplied by adherence to the Gospel, is added. Furthermore, the Gospel relaxes the Law's requirement of perfection; through pardon, God accepts our will to obey in the place of perfect obedience.

Lev 27:34

These are the commandments which the Lord commanded Moses for the children of Israel on Mount Sinai.

Deut 1:1–5

These are the words which Moses spoke to all Israel on this side of the Jordan in the wilderness, in the plain opposite Suph, between Paran, Tophel, Laban, Hazeroth, and Dizahab. ²It is eleven days' journey from Horeb by way of Mount Seir to Kadesh Barnea. ³Now it came to pass in the fortieth year, in the eleventh month, on the first day of the month, that Moses spoke to the children of Israel according to all that the Lord had given him as commandments to them, ⁴after he had killed Sihon king of the Amorites, who dwelt in Heshbon, and Og king of Bashan, who dwelt at Ashtaroth in Edrei. ⁵On this side of the Jordan in the land of Moab, Moses began to explain this law, saying, . . .

Deut 4:44–49

Now this is the law which Moses set before the children of Israel. ⁴⁵These are the testimonies, the statutes, and the judgments which Moses spoke to the children of Israel after they came out of Egypt, ⁴⁶on this side of the Jordan, in the valley opposite Beth Peor, in the land of Sihon king of the Amorites, who dwelt at Heshbon, whom Moses and the children of Israel defeated after they came out of Egypt. ⁴⁷And they took possession of his land and the land of Og king of Bashan, two kings of the Amorites, who were on this side of the Jordan, toward the rising of the sun, ⁴⁸from Aroer, which is on the bank of the River Arnon, even to Mount Sion (that is, Hermon), ⁴⁹and all the plain on the east side of the Jordan as far as the Sea of the Arabah, below the slopes of Pisgah.

Deut 29:1

These are the words of the covenant which the Lord commanded Moses to make with the children of Israel in the land of Moab, besides the covenant which He made with them in Horeb.

- Moses subdues the people to obedience with praises and commendations of the Law.
- The reference to another "covenant . . . besides the covenant . . . made with them in Horeb" is not to any substantive additions to the Decalogue but to the further explanations of it just given by Moses (essentially chapters 1–28 of Deuteronomy). This explanatory "covenant" was added lest the brevity of Horeb's pronouncements render it obscure to an ignorant and slow-hearted people. Moreover, as a new generation was about to enter the Promised Land, God *renews* the covenant of the previous generation.

First Commandment

You shall have no other gods before Me.

General Principle: *We must not worship any but Jehovah.*

Exod 20:3

You shall have no other gods before Me.

Deut 5:7

You shall have no other gods before Me.

- No gods may be opposed to the true and only God.
- We defile and corrupt true religion when God's glory is diminished in the least degree.
- The literal Hebrew reads "no other gods before my face."
- This commandment comprehends the inward worship of God (external idolatry is the second commandment).
- Only God, not figments of our imagination, may be worshipped.

Exposition

Deut 6:4, 13

Hear, O Israel: The Lord our God, the Lord is one! . . . ¹³ You shall fear the Lord your God and serve Him.

Deut 10:20

You shall fear the Lord your God; you shall serve Him, and to Him you shall hold fast.

Deut 6:16

You shall not tempt the Lord your God as you tempted Him in Massah.

- God has the sole ("one") power and glory and is alone to be worshiped.
- Since he is the only God, we must worship him undividedly.
- He commands voluntary reverence that is demonstrated in worship.

- We must not depart from him in the slightest, avoiding all corrupt worship.
- God's peculiar attributes must be acknowledged.
- We must believe in his providential care.

Lev 19:1–2

And the Lord spoke to Moses, saying, ²"Speak to all the congregation of the children of Israel, and say to them: 'You shall be holy, for I the Lord your God am holy.'"

- God's nature is the standard of our service to him.
- We should study to be holy.

Deut 6:14–15

You shall not go after other gods, the gods of the peoples who are all around you ¹⁵(for the Lord your God is a jealous God among you), lest the anger of the Lord your God be aroused against you and destroy you from the face of the earth.

- God establishes his authority alone so that the common belief of the Gentiles might be despised.
- Threats are added. His jealousy permits no rival and the nearness of his presence inspires terror and reproves the ingratitude of seeking gods afar off.

Deut 18:9–14

When you come into the land which the Lord your God is giving you, you shall not learn to follow the abominations of those nations. ¹⁰There shall not be found among you anyone who makes his son or his daughter pass through the fire, or one who practices witchcraft, or a soothsayer, or one who interprets omens, or a sorcerer, ¹¹or one who conjures spells, or a medium, or a spiritist, or one who calls up the dead. ¹²For all who do these things are an abomination to the Lord, and because of these abominations the Lord your God drives them out from before you. ¹³You shall be blameless before the Lord your God. ¹⁴For these nations which you will dispossess listened to soothsayers and diviners; but as for you, the Lord your God has not appointed such for you.

- We are not to mix up the worship of God with the inventions of men.
- Our natural desire for knowledge gets corrupted by two errors: to know more than has been revealed and to seek knowledge illicitly.
- God condemns these practices: (a) burning children, sometimes even to death, as propitious sacrifices to gods; (b) augury, astrology; (c) divination, soothsaying; (d) jugglery (deceiving by sleight of hand); (e) enchantments, magic arts; (f) witchcraft, fortune-telling; (g) wizardry (claiming special knowledge for deceit); (h) necromancy (prophesying upon the answers of the dead).
- We must avoid the sins of unbelievers that provoke God to judgment.
- Our worship should be "blameless," that is, with no corruptions that draw us away from the one true God.
- Israel's religion was not to follow the superstitious defilements of the Canaanite nations.

Deut 18:15–18

The Lord your God will raise up for you a Prophet like me from your midst, from your brethren. Him you shall hear, ¹⁶according to all you desired of the Lord your God in Horeb in the day of the assembly, saying, "Let me not hear again the voice of the Lord my God, nor let me see this great fire anymore, lest I die." ¹⁷And the Lord said to me: "What they have spoken is good. ¹⁸I will raise up for them a Prophet like you from among their brethren, and will put My words in His mouth, and He shall speak to them all that I command Him."

- "A Prophet" is an enallage (grammatical substitution) for a number of prophets.
- The doctrine of the Prophets should alone have force among Israel. Hearkening unto the prophetic word should be the continual manner of the church's government.
- Christ ultimately fulfills and ends the prophetic office (Heb 1:1–2).
- The comparison to Moses is to ensure the coming prophets' authority, since Moses' authority was not questioned.
- Convinced of their weakness, at Mount Sinai the Jews themselves asked for prophets.
- The prophetical teaching office is a sign of God's favor.

DEUT 13:1-4

If there arises among you a prophet or a dreamer of dreams, and he gives you a sign or a wonder, ²and the sign or the wonder comes to pass, of which he spoke to you, saying, "Let us go after other gods"—which you have not known—"and let us serve them," ³you shall not listen to the words of that prophet or that dreamer of dreams, for the LORD your God is testing you to know whether you love the LORD your God with all your heart and with all your soul. ⁴You shall walk after the LORD your God and fear Him, and keep His commandments and obey His voice; you shall serve Him and hold fast to Him.

DEUT 18:21-22

And if you say in your heart, "How shall we know the word which the LORD has not spoken?"—²²when a prophet speaks in the name of the LORD, if the thing does not happen or come to pass, that is the thing which the LORD has not spoken; the prophet has spoken it presumptuously; you shall not be afraid of him.

- The Law, as the Gospel (Eph 4:14), was given to keep the church pure by exposing imposters within its ranks.
- God sometimes allows Satan's ministers to predict events (e.g., Balaam).
- Imposters who work miracles are servants of God's vengeance to ensnare rebels (2 Thess 2:10-12).
- False signs test, that is, lay open what was before concealed. As in the case of Abraham, testing separates hypocrites from true believers (this is also a function of heresies, 1 Cor 11:19).
- People who may at times prophesy correctly do not always deliver true revelations (e.g., Caiaphas).
- Ordinarily, claims to prophet-hood are tested by fulfilled predictions (see Jer 28:8-9).
- Signs inseparably connect to righteous doctrine, as aids to faith.
- True prophets are indicated by fulfilled prophesy along with right doctrine.

LEV 18:21

And you shall not let any of your descendants pass through the fire to Molech, nor shall you profane the name of your God: I am the LORD.

LEV 19:26, 31

Nor shall you practice divination or soothsaying. . . . ³¹Give no regard to mediums and familiar spirits; do not seek after them, to be defiled by them: I am the LORD your God.

DEUT 12:29–32

When the LORD your God cuts off from before you the nations which you go to dispossess, and you displace them and dwell in their land, ³⁰take heed to yourself that you are not ensnared to follow them, after they are destroyed from before you, and that you do not inquire after their gods, saying, "How did these nations serve their gods? I also will do likewise." ³¹You shall not worship the LORD your God in that way; for every abomination to the LORD which He hates they have done to their gods; for they burn even their sons and daughters in the fire to their gods. ³²Whatever I command you, be careful to observe it; you shall not add to it nor take away from it.

- God condemns these practices: (a) adulterous sacrifices, especially Molech worship that causes children to pass through fire; (b) heeding false revelations via auguries, divinations, witchcraft, magic, or enchantments.
- "I am the Lord" declarations were meant to sanctify him, and thus his people, from idols.
- Do not inquire into the religious practices of pagans or be enticed by such novelties.
- By forbidding the adding to or subtracting from his Law, we learn that whatever men invent God condemns.

POLITICAL SUPPLEMENTS

DEUT 18:19

And it shall be that whoever will not hear My words, which He speaks in My name, I will require it of him.

DEUT 13:5

But that prophet or that dreamer of dreams shall be put to death, because he has spoken in order to turn you away from the LORD your God, who brought you out of the land of Egypt and redeemed you from the house of bondage, to entice you from the way in which the LORD *your God commanded you to walk. So you shall put away the evil from your midst.*

- These are political punishments for rebelliously violating God's religion.
- God threatens with destruction whoever refuses to obey his prophets' commands.
- The true God and his true religion are in view, not theism in general or any other superstition.
- Instigation to apostasy (i.e., to pluck up religion by the roots) is a capital offense. Trifling errors such as simply spreading false doctrine are not included in this penal sanction.
- Such severe punishments can be given only in a society where: (a) true religion has been positively established by public consent and the vote of the people; (b) indisputable proofs of God's nature and how he is to be worshiped has been sufficiently manifested from his Law.
- Such punishments should not be rushed into with rash and inconsiderate zeal, but with a careful examination.
- A magistracy that defends and provides for the tranquility and safety of the church is not changing the spiritual nature of Christ's kingdom. Christ is bringing kings under his subjection, taming their violence, and converting them from cruel persecutors into patrons and guardians of his church (Isa 49:6, 23; 1 Tim 2:2).
- Magistrates who allow instigators to apostasy to go unpunished count the salvation of those souls for nothing.

DEUT 17:12–13

Now the man who acts presumptuously and will not heed the priest who stands to minister there before the LORD *your God, or the judge, that man shall die. So you shall put away the evil from Israel.* ¹³*And all the people shall hear and fear, and no longer act presumptuously.*

- What was said above about stubbornly ignoring the prophets is now extended to the judgment of priests.
- Unqualified obedience to rulers of the church is not commanded, but only to lawful orders. The traitor priest, Urijah, was to be dis-

obeyed in his commands for profane offerings (2 Kgs 16:12). The prophets also waged open war with rebellious priests.

- Execution was not simply to the disobedient, but to those presumptuously and arrogantly disobedient.

- Execution was to deter presumptuousness. Impunity baits to sin and nurses unbridled licentiousness leading eventually to the destruction of the church.

DEUT 13:6–11

If your brother, the son of your mother, your son or your daughter, the wife of your bosom, or your friend who is as your own soul, secretly entices you, saying, "Let us go and serve other gods," which you have not known, neither you nor your fathers, ⁷of the gods of the people which are all around you, near to you or far off from you, from one end of the earth to the other end of the earth, ⁸you shall not consent to him or listen to him, nor shall your eye pity him, nor shall you spare him or conceal him; ⁹but you shall surely kill him; your hand shall be first against him to put him to death, and afterward the hand of all the people. ¹⁰And you shall stone him with stones until he dies, because he sought to entice you away from the LORD your God, who brought you out of the land of Egypt, from the house of bondage. ¹¹So all Israel shall hear and fear, and not again do such wickedness as this among you.

- Even secret (i.e., within individual houses) instigation to apostasy is a capital offense.

- Again, this applies only where true religion is duly constituted, and not for trifling errors, but against apostates who adulterate God's worship or abolish pure doctrine.

- God requires a zeal for religion not dissuaded by tears, allurements, or sadness that accompanies the sight of punishment of those close to us. Otherwise we set our affections against God [cf. Matt 10:37].

- The severity of punishment is on account of our natural slackness to avenge the insults toward God, and because more harmful diseases require such. Moreover, since Israel was surrounded by idolaters, and since men commonly produce conformity of habits by intercommunication, and since, due to our depraved nature, the worse generally pervert the better, such a severe penalty is merited.

- The witnesses should throw the first stone at criminals condemned in public trials (vigilante justice is thus not sanctioned). This provision makes accusers more cautious and moderate in giving their testimony.
- Ingratitude for God's redemption aggravates this crime.
- Deterrence, again, is a purpose for this punishment.

DEUT 13:12–17

If you hear someone in one of your cities, which the LORD your God gives you to dwell in, saying, ^{13}"Corrupt men have gone out from among you and enticed the inhabitants of their city, saying, 'Let us go and serve other gods'"—which you have not known— ^{14}then you shall inquire, search out, and ask diligently. And if it is indeed true and certain that such an abomination was committed among you, ^{15}you shall surely strike the inhabitants of that city with the edge of the sword, utterly destroying it, all that is in it and its livestock—with the edge of the sword. ^{16}And you shall gather all its plunder into the middle of the street, and completely burn with fire the city and all its plunder, for the LORD your God. It shall be a heap forever; it shall not be built again. ^{17}So none of the accursed things shall remain in your hand, that the LORD may turn from the fierceness of His anger and show you mercy, have compassion on you and multiply you, just as He swore to your fathers, . . .

- This punishment, like the previous ones, can only be resorted to where true religion is received by common consent and proved on solid grounds.
- The crime is openly paraded ("gone out from among you").
- The crime was unpardonable, being committed by those educated in the Law (thus not involuntarily deceived), who had grown weary of religion and set their hearts on the impostures of the devil.
- Let us learn from this grim punishment how God detests the crime of setting up false and spurious modes of worship.
- The whole city, including even infants, being wholly given over to the ban, must be destroyed to propitiate God's wrath lest it be poured out on the whole nation.

EXOD 22:18

You shall not permit a sorceress to live.

LEV 20:6, 27

And the person who turns to mediums and familiar spirits, to prostitute himself with them, I will set My face against that person and cut him off from his people. . . . ²⁷A man or a woman who is a medium, or who has familiar spirits, shall surely be put to death; they shall stone them with stones. Their blood shall be upon them.

NUM 15:30–31

But the person who does anything presumptuously, whether he is native-born or a stranger, that one brings reproach on the LORD, and he shall be cut off from among his people. ³¹Because he has despised the word of the LORD, and has broken His commandment, that person shall be completely cut off; his guilt shall be upon him.

LEV 20:1–5

Then the LORD spoke to Moses, saying, ²"Again, you shall say to the children of Israel: 'Whoever of the children of Israel, or of the strangers who dwell in Israel, who gives any of his descendants to Molech, he shall surely be put to death. The people of the land shall stone him with stones. ³I will set My face against that man, and will cut him off from his people, because he has given some of his descendants to Molech, to defile My sanctuary and profane My holy name. ⁴And if the people of the land should in any way hide their eyes from the man, when he gives some of his descendants to Molech, and they do not kill him, ⁵then I will set My face against that man and against his family; and I will cut him off from his people, and all who prostitute themselves with him to commit harlotry with Molech.'"

EXOD 12:15, 19

Whoever eats leavened bread from the first day until the seventh day, that person shall be cut off from Israel. . . . ¹⁹Whoever eats what is leavened, that same person shall be cut off from the congregation of Israel, whether he is a stranger or a native of the land.

- Here the Lord wills punishments for introducing corruptions into religion, even though religion may not be professedly forsaken.

- Witches are to be executed by stoning—included are enchantresses, sorceresses, and devotees to magic designed to injure persons or to seek revelations from Satan.
- Numbers 15:30–31 does not envision second table crimes but those committed against worship. Arrogantly inventing unlawful worship practices profanes God's true and legitimate worship and despises his Word.
- Molech worship (viz., sacrificing children) gives to him the seed that God adopts to himself and seeks to blot out this grace of adoption. Such practices merit execution by stoning. If magistrates connive at this crime, God will himself more severely punish the criminals and will also implicate these negligent magistrates in his wrath.
- As the Passover rite kept the people's redemption in memory, and as political laws sanction worship by punishments, eating leavened bread in Passover was a gross crime punished politically.

Deut 17:14–20

When you come to the land which the Lord your God is giving you, and possess it and dwell in it, and say, "I will set a king over me like all the nations that are around me," [15]you shall surely set a king over you whom the Lord your God chooses; one from among your brethren you shall set as king over you; you may not set a foreigner over you, who is not your brother. [16]But he shall not multiply horses for himself, nor cause the people to return to Egypt to multiply horses, for the Lord has said to you, "You shall not return that way again." [17]Neither shall he multiply wives for himself, lest his heart turn away; nor shall he greatly multiply silver and gold for himself. [18]Also it shall be, when he sits on the throne of his kingdom, that he shall write for himself a copy of this law in a book, from the one before the priests, the Levites. [19]And it shall be with him, and he shall read it all the days of his life, that he may learn to fear the Lord his God and be careful to observe all the words of this law and these statutes, [20]that his heart may not be lifted above his brethren, that he may not turn aside from the commandment to the right hand or to the left, and that he may prolong his days in his kingdom, he and his children in the midst of Israel.

- Kings are regulated that they might not depart and lead the people away from devotion to God.

- This passage concerns the time when the monarchy age arrives. Israel is warned that adopting the government form of other nations might beget the likeness of other pagan practices as well.

- Although God planned very early to set up David as a *kingly* type of Christ (see Gen 49:10), the people's perverse desire to emulate the pagans hastened the order of things, and for this reason God ascribes the beginning of the kingdom to them.

- Kings must be chosen from among the church so that pure religion is maintained in the land, and that outsiders not impose foreign gods by royal power.

- Kings were: (a) prohibited from multiplying horses, that a prideful desire might not ensue to invade Egypt; (b) prohibited from polygamy, that he might be an example to the common folk; (c) cautioned against royal splendor disposing him to intemperance; (d) prohibited from multiplying treasures, since they could not come but by violent and unjust taxes, and might encourage unjust warfare and gross dissipations.

- The Mosaic Law was copied and ceremoniously presented to the king, that he might know his civil duties, that he might fear God, and that he learn not to exalt himself tyrannously above the people.

- Reigns would be prolonged by lawful obedience.

Deut 20:1–4

When you go out to battle against your enemies, and see horses and chariots and people more numerous than you, do not be afraid of them; for the Lord your God is with you, who brought you up from the land of Egypt. ²So it shall be, when you are on the verge of battle, that the priest shall approach and speak to the people. ³And he shall say to them, "Hear, O Israel: Today you are on the verge of battle with your enemies. Do not let your heart faint, do not be afraid, and do not tremble or be terrified because of them; ⁴for the Lord your God is He who goes with you, to fight for you against your enemies, to save you."

- Even in warfare we must trust God for help and follow his ways.
- Even though God forbade Israel the cavalry strength of other nations (Deut 17:16; Ps 20:7; Isa 31:1), they should not fear because the same redemptive power manifested against Egypt will be displayed against aggressors.
- Priests encouraged the troops by reminding them of God's presence.
- By God's many admonitions against fear we learn how difficult it is to cure this evil.

NUM 10:1–10

And the LORD spoke to Moses, saying: ²"Make two silver trumpets for yourself; you shall make them of hammered work; you shall use them for calling the congregation and for directing the movement of the camps. ³When they blow both of them, all the congregation shall gather before you at the door of the tabernacle of meeting. ⁴But if they blow only one, then the leaders, the heads of the divisions of Israel, shall gather to you. ⁵When you sound the advance, the camps that lie on the east side shall then begin their journey. ⁶When you sound the advance the second time, then the camps that lie on the south side shall begin their journey; they shall sound the call for them to begin their journeys. ⁷And when the assembly is to be gathered together, you shall blow, but not sound the advance. ⁸The sons of Aaron, the priests, shall blow the trumpets; and these shall be to you as an ordinance forever throughout your generations. ⁹When you go to war in your land against the enemy who oppresses you, then you shall sound an alarm with the trumpets, and you will be remembered before the LORD your God, and you will be saved from your enemies. ¹⁰Also in the day of your gladness, in your appointed feasts, and at the beginning of your months, you shall blow the trumpets over your burnt offerings and over the sacrifices of your peace offerings; and they shall be a memorial for you before your God: I am the LORD your God."

- Trumpets giving a gathering-signal taught the people always to be attentive to God's voice, that they should not go to battle except in reliance on God's aid, and that they should account all their strength the result of his grace (Ps 33:16, 18).

- The trumpets' uses: (a) gathering the rulers and people to public assemblies; (b) alarming them of enemy aggressors; (c) announcing sacrifices and festivals.
- Having assemblies called by priests shows us that God considers all assemblies accursed where he does not preside by his Word.
- The trumpets sounding once called forth princes or heads of households. The sound doubled to call the whole people. And distinctive sounds were given to either side of the camp to advance for battle.
- God would look upon obedience to the trumpet commands and honor it with his paternal favor.

Second Commandment

You shall not make for yourself a carved image—any likeness of anything that is in heaven above, or that is in the earth beneath, or that is in the water under the earth; you shall not bow down to them nor serve them. For I, the L<small>ORD</small> your God, am a jealous God, visiting the iniquity of the fathers upon the children to the third and fourth generations of those who hate Me, but showing mercy to thousands, to those who love Me and keep My commandments.

General Principle: *We must not legitimate worship that is the inventions of men.*

Exod 20:4–6

You shall not make for yourself a carved image—any likeness of anything that is in heaven above, or that is in the earth beneath, or that is in the water under the earth; [5] you shall not bow down to them nor serve them. For I, the Lord your God, am a jealous God, visiting the iniquity of the fathers upon the children to the third and fourth generations of those who hate Me, [6] but showing mercy to thousands, to those who love Me and keep My commandments.

Deut 5:8–10

You shall not make for yourself a carved image—any likeness of anything that is in heaven above, or that is in the earth beneath, or that is in the water under the earth; [9] you shall not bow down to them nor serve them. For I, the Lord your God, am a jealous God, visiting the iniquity of the fathers upon the children to the third and fourth generations of those who hate Me, [10] but showing mercy to thousands, to those who love Me and keep My commandments.

- God condemns all human fabrications of worship.
- It is wrong to seek the presence of God in any visible image and even to make an image of him. The making of the image very often leads to worshiping it.
- This commandment is not condemning all pictures and sculptures. God seeks here only to rescue his glory from all corrupting imaginations.
- Fashioning the image itself denies the true God. So false religionists are condemned who claim they only worship the God represented in the image and not the representation itself.

- God here partly terrorizes to obedience with threats, partly allures by promises. These extend even to posterity.
- God is jealous for purity and likens worshiping idols to violating a marriage covenant.
- God shows *mercy* even to those who love him and keep his laws. This sufficiently precludes any supposed merits of men.
- Keeping God's commandments flow from a love of him, giving proof of the love.
- God's promise to bless a thousand generations is not absolute to every descendent. The fruits of this promised grace, however, are manifested in temporal blessings, and often remained during disobedience. Abraham's seed was left the Law, prophets, and temple even in their apostasy, so long as God saw fit.
- God identifies transgressors as haters of him.
- As all are under condemnation, God can and has judged children for the sins of their fathers. The Canaanites who were guilty at the time of Abraham [Gen 15:16] nonetheless had their punishment inflicted on a later generation. Israel of Christ's day had guilt of all the previous generations imputed to them (Matt 23:35). If we struggle to understand how God deals with everyone according to his deserts and yet visits the sins of the fathers upon the children, let us recall that God's judgments are incomprehensible. But often the punishment is upon those who are imitators of their father's sin, not innocent children.
- This promise is common to the whole first table, not to the commandment itself, thus not contradicting Paul's statement in Ephesians 6:2 that the fifth commandment is the first with a promise.

Exposition

Exod 34:17

You shall make no molded gods for yourselves.

Lev 19:4

Do not turn to idols, nor make for yourselves molded gods: I am the Lord your God.

Lev 26:1

You shall not make idols for yourselves; neither a carved image nor a sacred pillar shall you rear up for yourselves; nor shall you set up an engraved stone in your land, to bow down to it; for I am the Lord your God.

Exod 20:22–23

Then the Lord said to Moses, "Thus you shall say to the children of Israel: 'You have seen that I have talked with you from heaven. ²³You shall not make anything to be with Me—gods of silver or gods of gold you shall not make for yourselves.'"

- "I am the Lord your God" is mentioned as a reminder that we despoil his honor whenever we devise anything earthly of him.
- That God "talked . . . from heaven" explains why erecting earthly images wrongly ties God down to corruptible materials.

Deut 4:12–19, 23–24

And the Lord spoke to you out of the midst of the fire. You heard the sound of the words, but saw no form; you only heard a voice. ¹³So He declared to you His covenant which He commanded you to perform, the Ten Commandments; and He wrote them on two tablets of stone. ¹⁴And the Lord commanded me at that time to teach you statutes and judgments, that you might observe them in the land which you cross over to possess. ¹⁵Take careful heed to yourselves, for you saw no form when the Lord spoke to you at Horeb out of the midst of the fire, ¹⁶lest you act corruptly and make for yourselves a carved image in the form of any figure: the likeness of male or female, ¹⁷the likeness of any animal that is on the earth or the likeness of any winged bird that flies in the air, ¹⁸the likeness of anything that creeps on the ground or the likeness of any fish that is in the water beneath the earth. ¹⁹And take heed, lest you lift your eyes to heaven, and when you see the sun, the moon, and the stars, all the host of heaven, you feel driven to worship them and serve them, which the Lord your God has given to all the peoples under the whole heaven as a heritage. . . . ²³Take heed to yourselves, lest you forget the covenant of the Lord your God which He made with you, and make for yourselves a carved image in the form of anything which the Lord your God has forbidden you. ²⁴For the Lord your God is a consuming fire, a jealous God.

Exod 34:14

. . . (for you shall worship no other god, for the Lord, whose name is Jealous, is a jealous God), . . .

Deut 11:16–17

Take heed to yourselves, lest your heart be deceived, and you turn aside and serve other gods and worship them, ¹⁷lest the Lord's anger be aroused against you, and He shut up the heavens so that there be no rain, and the land yield no produce, and you perish quickly from the good land which the Lord is giving you.

Deut 8:19–20

Then it shall be, if you by any means forget the Lord your God, and follow other gods, and serve them and worship them, I testify against you this day that you shall surely perish. ²⁰As the nations which the Lord destroys before you, so you shall perish, because you would not be obedient to the voice of the Lord your God.

- God's manifestation by a voice and not in bodily form confirms the prohibition of the second commandment.
- Those not content with God's voice but seek his visible form, substitute imaginations and phantoms in his place. Though God has at times manifested himself in visible forms, these were peculiar circumstances, not a general rule. These forms were intended to elevate men's minds to things above.
- This prohibition cannot be restricted to the ancient Jews, as Paul reasons from the common origin of our nature (Acts 17:29), and John likewise warns New Covenant believers (1 John 5:21). Also, it is madness to take away one of the ten laws.
- God reproves the absurdity of worshiping the heavenly bodies since they were given to serve us.
- God issues threats to incline our minds to obedience, speaking of his vengeance as a consuming fire.
- Moses warns us ("lest your heart be deceived") that without diligence we become easily susceptible to this snare of Satan.
- God declares all apostates who do not confine themselves to the simplicity of his Law.

- Social, political, and economic threats are affixed to prohibitions of idolatry.

DEUT 16:22

You shall not set up a sacred pillar, which the LORD your God hates.

EXOD 23:24

You shall not bow down to their gods, nor serve them, nor do according to their works; . . .

- False images of God are prohibited, not images or statues in general. They are false because God has no bodily form and therefore they dishonor his glory.
- Israel's worship must be separated from all Gentile superstitions.
- The prohibition "nor do according to [the Gentile's] works" proves that all corrupt worship is comprehended under the term idolatry.

DEUT 12:4–14, 17–18, 26–27

You shall not worship the LORD your God with such things. ⁵But you shall seek the place where the LORD your God chooses, out of all your tribes, to put His name for His dwelling place; and there you shall go. ⁶There you shall take your burnt offerings, your sacrifices, your tithes, the heave offerings of your hand, your vowed offerings, your freewill offerings, and the firstborn of your herds and flocks. ⁷And there you shall eat before the LORD your God, and you shall rejoice in all to which you have put your hand, you and your households, in which the LORD your God has blessed you. ⁸You shall not at all do as we are doing here today—every man doing whatever is right in his own eyes—⁹for as yet you have not come to the rest and the inheritance which the LORD your God is giving you. ¹⁰But when you cross over the Jordan and dwell in the land which the LORD your God is giving you to inherit, and He gives you rest from all your enemies round about, so that you dwell in safety, ¹¹then there will be the place where the LORD your God chooses to make His name abide. There you shall bring all that I command you: your burnt offerings, your sacrifices, your tithes, the heave offerings of your hand, and all your choice offerings which you vow to the LORD. ¹²And you shall rejoice before the LORD your God, you and your sons and your daughters, your male and female servants, and the Levite who is within your gates, since he has no portion nor inheritance with you. ¹³Take heed to yourself that you do not offer your burnt offerings in every place that you see; ¹⁴but in the place which the Lord *chooses, in one of your tribes, there you shall offer your burnt offerings, and there you shall do all that I command you. . . . ¹⁷You may not eat within your gates the tithe of your grain or your new wine or your oil, of the firstborn of your herd or your flock, of any of your offerings which you vow, of your freewill offerings, or of the heave offering of your hand. ¹⁸But you must eat them before the* Lord *your God in the place which the* Lord *your God chooses, you and your son and your daughter, your male servant and your female servant, and the Levite who is within your gates; and you shall rejoice before the* Lord *your God in all to which you put your hands. . . . ²⁶Only the holy things which you have, and your vowed offerings, you shall take and go to the place which the* Lord *chooses. ²⁷And you shall offer your burnt offerings, the meat and the blood, on the altar of the* Lord *your God; and the blood of your sacrifices shall be poured out on the altar of the* Lord *your God, and you shall eat the meat.*

- Having one sanctuary and one altar symbolized the difference between God and all idols and between legitimate worship and fictitious rites.
- The one altar also sought to instill in believers a care for the unity of the faith.
- God commends obedience by claiming the right and authority to choose the place of worship.
- Jerusalem became the chosen place, chosen at David's time. Until then, worship was to be in the sanctuary (i.e., where the Ark presided), wherever its various lodgings.
- For the labor and expense of journeying to the Ark for sacrifices, God promises a compensation to them in that they may feast, partaking of what is left of the sacrificed animals.
- The "tithes" noted do not refer to the general tithes (those given by the people to the Levites), but to the special tithe of that general tithe (that given by the Levites to the priests) [see Num 18:25–30]. Otherwise the families of the Levites dispersed throughout the Land would be without food.

- "Every man doing whatever is right in his own eyes" refers not to inventions of men, but to the unfixed location of sacrifices pre-Promised Land.
- God will choose the fixed place of worship when he gives rest from all surrounding enemies, which rest came in David's time.

DEUT 14:23–26

And you shall eat before the LORD your God, in the place where He chooses to make His name abide, the tithe of your grain and your new wine and your oil, of the firstborn of your herds and your flocks, that you may learn to fear the LORD your God always. ²⁴But if the journey is too long for you, so that you are not able to carry the tithe, or if the place where the LORD your God chooses to put His name is too far from you, when the LORD your God has blessed you, ²⁵then you shall exchange it for money, take the money in your hand, and go to the place which the LORD your God chooses. ²⁶And you shall spend that money for whatever your heart desires: for oxen or sheep, for wine or similar drink, for whatever your heart desires; you shall eat there before the LORD your God, and you shall rejoice, you and your household.

- The "tithe" here refers to vows and free gifts that were to be brought to the appointed place, not referring to the general Levitical tithe. If the general tithe was to be taken to Jerusalem then the Levites who were dispersed abroad would be without subsistence.
- For those too far from the appointed place, they might exchange their offerings for money. This money in turn could buy in Jerusalem whatever was vowed or freely offered.

EXOD 20:24–25

An altar of earth you shall make for Me, and you shall sacrifice on it your burnt offerings and your peace offerings, your sheep and your oxen. In every place where I record My name I will come to you, and I will bless you. ²⁵And if you make Me an altar of stone, you shall not build it of hewn stone; for if you use your tool on it, you have profaned it.

DEUT 27:5–7

And there you shall build an altar to the LORD your God, an altar of stones; you shall not use an iron tool on them. ⁶You shall build with whole stones the altar of the LORD your God, and offer burnt offerings on it to the LORD your God. ⁷*You shall offer peace offerings, and shall eat there, and rejoice before the* LORD *your God.*

- Before the perpetual worship place is revealed, altars were to be made of earth or of stones without tools. In this way, they would fall down of themselves so that they may not be permanent structures. Otherwise posterity may be enticed to superstition, unduly fixing special reverence upon places dedicated by the fathers. For this reason, the 9½ tribes gathered for war against the 2½ tribes east of the Jordan River because of the lasting altar they built (Josh 22). The 2½ tribes were cleared of rebellion when once it was explained that the altar was a memorial of brotherly union with the 9½, not an altar for sacrifices.
- That peace offerings can be offered on these altars shows that God will be favorable to those who obey his instructions on worship.

POLITICAL SUPPLEMENTS

EXOD 23:24

You shall utterly overthrow them and completely break down their sacred pillars.

DEUT 12:1–3

These are the statutes and judgments which you shall be careful to observe in the land which the LORD *God of your fathers is giving you to possess, all the days that you live on the earth. ²You shall utterly destroy all the places where the nations which you shall dispossess served their gods, on the high mountains and on the hills and under every green tree. ³And you shall destroy their altars, break their sacred pillars, and burn their wooden images with fire; you shall cut down the carved images of their gods and destroy their names from that place.*

EXOD 34:13

But you shall destroy their altars, break their sacred pillars, and cut down their wooden images . . .

DEUT 7:5

But thus you shall deal with them: you shall destroy their altars, and break down their sacred pillars, and cut down their wooden images, and burn their carved images with fire.

Num 33:52

Destroy all their engraved stones, destroy all their molded images, and demolish all their high places; . . .

Deut 16:21

You shall not plant for yourself any tree, as a wooden image, near the altar which you build for yourself to the Lord your God.

- These political enforcements against idolatry forced the people to take more diligent heed.
- Though what tends to foster superstition should be removed from society, there should be nowadays no scruples in retaining temples that had been polluted by idols and putting them to godly use.
- This destruction is directed to public authority, not private individuals, denoted by the phrase "to possess." In other words, when the people possessed the Land, the civil authorities had the charge of regulating such public interests.
- Not all statues are condemned, but only those that are intended to be a likeness of God erected for worship.
- The prohibition of planting trees near God's altar prevented imitating pagan rites and mingling them in with their own. For among the heathens, groves were sacred, and no religious object would receive reverence unless under the shade of trees. This regulation was all too necessary (see Isa 57:5; Jer 2:20; 3:6).

Exod 34:11–12, 15–16

Observe what I command you this day. Behold, I am driving out from before you the Amorite and the Canaanite and the Hittite and the Perizzite and the Hivite and the Jebusite. ¹²Take heed to yourself, lest you make a covenant with the inhabitants of the land where you are going, lest it be a snare in your midst. . . . ¹⁵lest you make a covenant with the inhabitants of the land, and they play the harlot with their gods and make sacrifice to their gods, and one of them invites you and you eat of his sacrifice, ¹⁶and you take of his daughters for your sons, and his daughters play the harlot with their gods and make your sons play the harlot with their gods.

Deut 7:1–4

When the Lord your God brings you into the land which you go to possess, and has cast out many nations before you, the Hittites and the

Girgashites and the Amorites and the Canaanites and the Perizzites and the Hivites and the Jebusites, seven nations greater and mightier than you, ²and when the LORD your God delivers them over to you, you shall conquer them and utterly destroy them. You shall make no covenant with them nor show mercy to them. ³Nor shall you make marriages with them. You shall not give your daughter to their son, nor take their daughter for your son. ⁴For they will turn your sons away from following Me, to serve other gods; so the anger of the LORD will be aroused against you and destroy you suddenly.

EXOD 23:31–33

For I will deliver the inhabitants of the land into your hand, and you shall drive them out before you. ³²You shall make no covenant with them, nor with their gods. ³³They shall not dwell in your land, lest they make you sin against Me. For if you serve their gods, it will surely be a snare to you.

- These passages are more apt under the second rather than the first commandment because God applies a remedy to external and manifest superstitions.

- Though from our own inner perversity we eagerly run into idolatry, this disease is increasingly inflamed when society allows idolatry with impunity, like a yoke that draws others along. Thus, that the church might preserve itself pure and devoted to God, he commanded that the inhabitants of Canaan be utterly destroyed.

- The Lord here forbids two kinds of covenants with unbelievers: (a) *Public* covenants between nations. Kings often compromise truth being fearful of portraying any disrespect to allied kings (see 2 Kgs 16:10). (b) *Private* covenants of marriage. Spouses notoriously lead their partners astray: women by their blandishments and men by their power.

- Though the general principle of these commandments still applies, this particular illustration does not. God does not now command us to put all the wicked to death; nor is a certain country assigned to the church to dwell apart from unbelievers and for the church to have dominion over it. The general principle, however, is that when the godly voluntarily yoke themselves with the ungodly they draw themselves to destruction (see 2 Cor 6:14). Not all contact,

- In order to engender courage and zeal, God adds a promise of victory over these nations. For though these nations far excelled them in power, numbers, and weaponry, God promised to conquer and give Israel all their vast lands. The Jews, then, out of gratitude, should follow their God after winning the war.

- Those who impugn God's justice in his command of holy war forget of whom they are speaking. The lands are his and thus he can give them to whomever he wills. Second, the peoples were wicked, and had been so for some time (see Gen 15:16). Wishing to show his vengeance, God can choose whatever agency he desires to execute it, and it is wicked to show mercy on those whom God wishes severity. Additionally, they become thorns and snares to whom unauthorized mercy has been shown (see Josh 23:13; Judges).

Deut 7:16–26

Also you shall destroy all the peoples whom the Lord *your God delivers over to you; your eye shall have no pity on them; nor shall you serve their gods, for that will be a snare to you. ¹⁷If you should say in your heart, "These nations are greater than I; how can I dispossess them?"— ¹⁸you shall not be afraid of them, but you shall remember well what the* Lord *your God did to Pharaoh and to all Egypt: ¹⁹the great trials which your eyes saw, the signs and the wonders, the mighty hand and the outstretched arm, by which the* Lord *your God brought you out. So shall the* Lord *your God do to all the peoples of whom you are afraid. ²⁰Moreover the* Lord *your God will send the hornet among them until those who are left, who hide themselves from you, are destroyed. ²¹You shall not be terrified of them; for the* Lord *your God, the great and awesome God, is among you. ²²And the* Lord *your God will drive out those nations before you little by little; you will be unable to destroy them at once, lest the beasts of the field become too numerous for you. ²³But the* Lord *your God will deliver them over to you, and will inflict defeat upon them until they are destroyed. ²⁴And He will deliver their kings into your hand, and you will destroy their name from under heaven; no one shall be able to stand against you until you have destroyed them. ²⁵You shall burn the carved*

though, is forbidden (1 Cor 5:10)—we must distinguish between contracts that associate us with them and those that do not diminish our liberty.

images of their gods with fire; you shall not covet the silver or gold that is on them, nor take it for yourselves, lest you be snared by it; for it is an abomination to the LORD your God. ²⁶Nor shall you bring an abomination into your house, lest you be doomed to destruction like it. You shall utterly detest it and utterly abhor it, for it is an accursed thing.

- In order to allay fears, God reminds his church what he had done on their behalf to mighty Egypt.
- God promises to send hornets to aid in Canaan's destruction (fulfillment noted in Josh 24:12).
- God's progressive destruction of Canaan was for the church's welfare, lest the land be overcome with wild beasts. So the prolongation of the war ought not trouble their minds or relax their zeal.
- The idols of precious metals were to be completely burned, not simply fashioned into something else. Furthermore, those touching the metals became polluted and accursed—not that the metals themselves were polluted, but they were in respect to the people who could not restrain their proclivities to idol worship. Hence God would have that to be abominable which in itself was pure. By this manner God related how greatly he despised idols.

DEUT 25:17–19

Remember what Amalek did to you on the way as you were coming out of Egypt, ¹⁸how he met you on the way and attacked your rear ranks, all the stragglers at your rear, when you were tired and weary; and he did not fear God. ¹⁹Therefore it shall be, when the LORD your God has given you rest from your enemies all around, in the land which the LORD your God is giving you to possess as an inheritance, that you will blot out the remembrance of Amalek from under heaven. You shall not forget.

- God enlists his army to exact vengeance upon the Amalekites, who merited such harshness because they deliberately rebelled against God ("did not fear God"), and for their cruelty among the Jews, their own kindred via Esau (see Gen 36:12). For in attempting to bring God's covenant to naught, having lost the status of the firstborn to Jacob, Esau's descendants sought to prevent Jacob's descendants from occupying the Promised Land—even attacking the invalids of the rear.

DEUT 23:3–8

An Ammonite or Moabite shall not enter the assembly of the LORD; even to the tenth generation none of his descendants shall enter the assembly of the LORD forever, ⁴because they did not meet you with bread and water on the road when you came out of Egypt, and because they hired against you Balaam the son of Beor from Pethor of Mesopotamia, to curse you. ⁵Nevertheless the LORD your God would not listen to Balaam, but the LORD your God turned the curse into a blessing for you, because the LORD your God loves you. ⁶You shall not seek their peace nor their prosperity all your days forever. ⁷You shall not abhor an Edomite, for he is your brother. You shall not abhor an Egyptian, because you were an alien in his land. ⁸The children of the third generation born to them may enter the assembly of the LORD.

- The Moabites and Ammonites are rejected from coming into the church because they refused to help their kindred Israel, and also hired a prophet to curse them. For their knowing and willing attempt to harm the church and to make God's salvific promise of no effect, they were justly disbarred from his sanctuary. This rejection, thus, has nothing to do with their incestuous origins.

- The Edomites, because of their close ancestry, and the Egyptians, because they had hosted the Jews, were allowed in the church in the third generation. For though Egypt cruelly oppressed them (yet in the beginning they allowed Israel to sojourn there rather than starve in Canaan, see Isa 52:4), and though Edom cruelly took up arms against Israel as did Moab, God reserves the right to have mercy upon whom he will have mercy.

DEUT 17:2–5, 7

If there is found among you, within any of your gates which the LORD your God gives you, a man or a woman who has been wicked in the sight of the LORD your God, in transgressing His covenant, ³who has gone and served other gods and worshiped them, either the sun or moon or any of the host of heaven, which I have not commanded, ⁴and it is told you, and you hear of it, then you shall inquire diligently. And if it is indeed true and certain that such an abomination has been committed in Israel, ⁵then you shall bring out to your gates that man or woman who has committed that wicked thing, and shall stone to death that man or woman with stones. . . . ⁷The hands of the witnesses shall be the first against him to put him to death, and afterward the hands of all the people. So you shall put away the evil from among you.

- The crime of idolatry differs from other crimes like theft, fornication, and drunkenness. It is not simply impiety, but covenant-breaking, whereby true religion is forsaken after men had professed devotion to God and had numbered themselves among his church.
- By synecdoche, all idolatry is included under "worshiped . . . sun or moon or any of the host of heaven." Likewise, cities are denoted by "gates."
- Judges are restrained from hasty condemnation and from idly and negligently passing over evidences that should be known. Moreover, that no crime may remain unpunished, judges are bidden to investigate all allegations.
- Stoning was the mode of capital punishments by the hands of the witnesses themselves, thereby deterring false and light accusations. Furthermore, as stoning required many hands, society as a whole declared their great indignation at the violation of God's worship.

Third Commandment

*You shall not take the name of the Lord your God in vain,
for the Lord will not hold him guiltless
who takes His name in vain.*

General Principle: *We must not irreverently or frivolously speak of God.*

Exod 20:7

You shall not take the name of the Lord your God in vain, for the Lord will not hold him guiltless who takes His name in vain.

Deut 5:11

You shall not take the name of the Lord your God in vain, for the Lord will not hold him guiltless who takes His name in vain.

- God must be greatly venerated in our speech.
- Here God's "name" cannot be restricted to Jehovah, as if God's majesty were confined to letters and syllables. God's name is as an image of his invisible essence. It is, in short, "what may be known of God" (Rom 1:19). For as Christ teaches that God's name is comprehended in the heavens, earth, temple, altar (Matt 5:34), we profane his name whenever we detract from his essence—his supreme wisdom, infinite power, justice, truth, clemency, or rectitude.
- Positively, the Lord here requires honest oath-taking, for it testifies to true piety. Negatively, the Lord here forbids deceitful oath-taking, lightly and disrespectfully citing the Name in proof of frivolous and trifling matters, and citing it in sport or derision.
- The punishment is added since sins of the tongue are difficult to restrain. God surely avenges contempt for his name.

Exposition

Lev 19:12

And you shall not swear by My name falsely, nor shall you profane the name of your God: I am the Lord.

Exod 23:13

And make no mention of the name of other gods, nor let it be heard from your mouth.

Deut 6:13

... shall take oaths in His name.

Deut 10:20

... take oaths in His name.

- While men wickedly defraud others, Moses warns against polluting and injuring God's name by adding perjury to fraud. For though men by perjury do harm to other men, they simultaneously disregard religion.
- Since God is eternal and immutable truth, he cannot be more grossly insulted than by being summoned as a witness to falsehood.
- In our oaths, God's name is first to be regarded as more precious than a hundred worlds.
- Swearing by other gods (as in Zeph 1:5) detracts from God's glory and seeks to transfer to others his sole rights.

Deut 23:21–23

When you make a vow to the Lord *your God, you shall not delay to pay it; for the* Lord *your God will surely require it of you, and it would be sin to you.* ^{22}*But if you abstain from vowing, it shall not be sin to you.* ^{23}*That which has gone from your lips you shall keep and perform, for you voluntarily vowed to the* Lord *your God what you have promised with your mouth.*

- Vowing is a kind of swearing to God. We take his name in vain when we renege on a promise made to him.
- Since vows are motivated by gratitude to God's goodness, it is sinful to fail to keep, through negligence and sloth, our end of the sacred engagement after God has been so good.
- Not all vows are included, but only lawful ones—manifest absurdities and evils otherwise result. God's Law, not our own fancies, are the standard of worship. So though many practices are

morally permissible (e.g., perpetual abstinence from meat), when offered as worship to God they become unlawful superstition. Unlawful vows also include promising God more than can be paid (e.g., perpetual celibacy by those not possessing the gift), or using the vow as an excuse for neglecting lawful duties.

- The keeping of vows is not meritorious.
- Though we are not duty-bound to make vows, God inculcates sobriety in making them inasmuch as we become doubly guilty if we choose to break the vow when it was an option not to vow (see Acts 5:4).
- A mutual agreement is required between the heart and tongue: when we utter a vow, we must delight in fulfilling it. We destroy God's beneficence when we turn paying vows into drudgery.

LEV 27:1–25, 27–29

Now the LORD spoke to Moses, saying, ²"Speak to the children of Israel, and say to them: 'When a man consecrates by a vow certain persons to the LORD, according to your valuation, ³if your valuation is of a male from twenty years old up to sixty years old, then your valuation shall be fifty shekels of silver, according to the shekel of the sanctuary. ⁴If it is a female, then your valuation shall be thirty shekels; ⁵and if from five years old up to twenty years old, then your valuation for a male shall be twenty shekels, and for a female ten shekels; ⁶and if from a month old up to five years old, then your valuation for a male shall be five shekels of silver, and for a female your valuation shall be three shekels of silver; ⁷and if from sixty years old and above, if it is a male, then your valuation shall be fifteen shekels, and for a female ten shekels. ⁸But if he is too poor to pay your valuation, then he shall present himself before the priest, and the priest shall set a value for him; according to the ability of him who vowed, the priest shall value him. ⁹If it is an animal that men may bring as an offering to the LORD, all that anyone gives to the LORD shall be holy. ¹⁰He shall not substitute it or exchange it, good for bad or bad for good; and if he at all exchanges animal for animal, then both it and the one exchanged for it shall be holy. ¹¹If it is an unclean animal which they do not offer as a sacrifice to the LORD, then he shall present the animal before the priest; ¹²and the priest shall set a value for it, whether it is good or bad; as you, the priest, value it, so it shall be. ¹³But if he wants at all to redeem it, then he must add one-fifth to your valuation. ¹⁴And when a man dedicates his house to be holy to the LORD, then the priest shall set a value for it, whether it is good or bad; as the priest values it, so it shall stand. ¹⁵If he who dedicated it wants to redeem his house, then he must add one-fifth of the money of your valuation to it, and it shall be his. ¹⁶If a man dedicates to the LORD part of a field of his possession, then your valuation shall be according to the seed for it. A homer of barley seed shall be valued at fifty shekels of silver. ¹⁷If he dedicates his field from the Year of Jubilee, according to your valuation it shall stand. ¹⁸But if he dedicates his field after the Jubilee, then the priest shall reckon to him the money due according to the years that remain till the Year of Jubilee, and it shall be deducted from your valuation. ¹⁹And if he who dedicates the field ever wishes to redeem it, then he must add one-fifth of the money of your valuation to it, and it shall belong to him. ²⁰But if he does not want to redeem the field, or if he has sold the field to another man, it shall not be redeemed anymore; ²¹but the field, when it is released in the Jubilee, shall be holy to the LORD, as a devoted field; it shall be the possession of the priest. ²²And if a man dedicates to the LORD a field which he has bought, which is not the field of his possession, ²³then the priest shall reckon to him the worth of your valuation, up to the Year of Jubilee, and he shall give your valuation on that day as a holy offering to the LORD. ²⁴In the Year of Jubilee the field shall return to him from whom it was bought, to the one who owned the land as a possession. ²⁵And all your valuations shall be according to the shekel of the sanctuary: twenty gerahs to the shekel. . . . ²⁷And if it is an unclean animal, then he shall redeem it according to your valuation, and shall add one-fifth to it; or if it is not redeemed, then it shall be sold according to your valuation. ²⁸Nevertheless no devoted offering that a man may devote to the LORD of all that he has, both man and beast, or the field of his possession, shall be sold or redeemed; every devoted offering is most holy to the LORD. ²⁹No person under the ban, who may become doomed to destruction among men, shall be redeemed, but shall surely be put to death.'"

- These verses show in what manner and at what price one may redeem what has been offered as a vow, supposing that the vows cannot be conveniently fulfilled.
- Some vows are a way of asking God to supply a lack (e.g., Hannah vowed to dedicate her son if God gave her one, 1 Sam 1:22), or to protect what seems in danger.

- The objects of vows may be ransomed back, according to: (a) the fixed values in the case of persons; or (b) the value assigned by the priest in the case of animals and property, plus 20 percent. In this way, rashness was punished and future inconsideration deterred. For the poor, the priest could fix an affordable price.

- The objects of vows were used for the temple or other religious exercises ("to the Lord"), thus the higher prices for men than women, and for those at more profitable ages.

- Moses treats of: (a) persons; (b) animals, clean for sacrificing and unclean for other uses (if the owner did not redeem them); (c) houses and lands.

- Clean animals given for sacrifice were not redeemable.

- Vowing land fraudulently was punished by forfeiture of the land to the priests forever, of which Moses compared to things placed under the ban.

- Proportioned to the time from the Year of Jubilee would land be estimated. At that fiftieth year, lands were restored to the possessors that poverty had driven out, lest God's partitioning of the Land through Joshua be obliterated.

- Lands were valued by the amount of seed its soil could take—fifty shekels of silver per homer of barley seed.

- Firstborns and tithes could not be vowed since they already belonged to God.

- Enemies of the church given over to the ban (e.g., Jericho) could not be redeemed.

Num 30:1–16

Then Moses spoke to the heads of the tribes concerning the children of Israel, saying, "This is the thing which the Lord has commanded: ²If a man makes a vow to the Lord, or swears an oath to bind himself by some agreement, he shall not break his word; he shall do according to all that proceeds out of his mouth. ³Or if a woman makes a vow to the Lord, and binds herself by some agreement while in her father's house in her youth, ⁴and her father hears her vow and the agreement by which she has bound herself, and her father holds his peace, then all her vows shall stand, and every agreement with which she has bound herself shall stand. ⁵But if her father overrules her on the day that he hears, then none of her vows nor her agreements by which she has bound herself shall stand; and the LORD *will release her, because her father overruled her. ⁶If indeed she takes a husband, while bound by her vows or by a rash utterance from her lips by which she bound herself, ⁷and her husband hears it, and makes no response to her on the day that he hears, then her vows shall stand, and her agreements by which she bound herself shall stand. ⁸But if her husband overrules her on the day that he hears it, he shall make void her vow which she took and what she uttered with her lips, by which she bound herself, and the* LORD *will release her. ⁹Also any vow of a widow or a divorced woman, by which she has bound herself, shall stand against her. ¹⁰If she vowed in her husband's house, or bound herself by an agreement with an oath, ¹¹and her husband heard it, and made no response to her and did not overrule her, then all her vows shall stand, and every agreement by which she bound herself shall stand. ¹²But if her husband truly made them void on the day he heard them, then whatever proceeded from her lips concerning her vows or concerning the agreement binding her, it shall not stand; her husband has made them void, and the* LORD *will release her. ¹³Every vow and every binding oath to afflict her soul, her husband may confirm it, or her husband may make it void. ¹⁴Now if her husband makes no response whatever to her from day to day, then he confirms all her vows or all the agreements that bind her; he confirms them, because he made no response to her on the day that he heard them. ¹⁵But if he does make them void after he has heard them, then he shall bear her guilt." ¹⁶These are the statutes which the* LORD *commanded Moses, between a man and his wife, and between a father and his daughter in her youth in her father's house.*

- Underlings' vows were subject to the consent of their covenant heads, whether father or husband. Consent could be by silence after hearing the vow.
- This rule probably applies to male children still under the authority of their fathers.
- Vows must be kept even when the underling's condition changes—for example, leaving a father's authority for a husband or becoming a widow or divorcee.
- When the covenant head voids the vow, the fact that Moses says "the Lord will release her" indicates that the vow was foolish thoughtlessness.

POLITICAL SUPPLEMENTS

Lev 24:15–16

Then you shall speak to the children of Israel, saying: "Whoever curses his God shall bear his sin. ¹⁶And whoever blasphemes the name of the Lord shall surely be put to death. All the congregation shall certainly stone him, the stranger as well as him who is born in the land. When he blasphemes the name of the Lord, he shall be put to death."

- "Cursing" means all profane and impure words that tend to brand with dishonor. It involves accusing God of injustice or cruelty, assailing him with blasphemies, designedly detracting from his glory, or scoffing at him.
- Such behavior is worthy of death, since the tongue, which was made to proclaim God's praises, insults him.
- The whole people participated in the execution that all may prove their zeal for his glory and that all may learn such monsters contaminate the earth.
- This penalty was for Jews and strangers alike.

Fourth Commandment

Remember the Sabbath day, to keep it holy. Six days you shall labor and do all your work, but the seventh day is the Sabbath of the LORD your God. In it you shall do no work: you, nor your son, nor your daughter, nor your male servant, nor your female servant, nor your cattle, nor your stranger who is within your gates. For in six days the LORD made the heavens and the earth, the sea, and all that is in them, and rested the seventh day. Therefore the LORD blessed the Sabbath day and hallowed it.

General Principle: *We must meditate on the works of God.*

Exod 20:8–11

Remember the Sabbath day, to keep it holy. ⁹Six days you shall labor and do all your work, ¹⁰but the seventh day is the Sabbath of the Lord your God. In it you shall do no work: you, nor your son, nor your daughter, nor your male servant, nor your female servant, nor your cattle, nor your stranger who is within your gates. ¹¹For in six days the Lord made the heavens and the earth, the sea, and all that is in them, and rested the seventh day. Therefore the Lord blessed the Sabbath day and hallowed it.

Deut 5:12–15

Observe the Sabbath day, to keep it holy, as the Lord your God commanded you. ¹³Six days you shall labor and do all your work, ¹⁴but the seventh day is the Sabbath of the Lord your God. In it you shall do no work: you, nor your son, nor your daughter, nor your male servant, nor your female servant, nor your ox, nor your donkey, nor any of your cattle, nor your stranger who is within your gates, that your male servant and your female servant may rest as well as you. ¹⁵And remember that you were a slave in the land of Egypt, and the Lord your God brought you out from there by a mighty hand and by an outstretched arm; therefore the Lord your God commanded you to keep the Sabbath day.

- The objective is to have believers exercise themselves in the worship of God, to divest of all reason and affections of the flesh.
- The fact that God notes as the perfection of sanctity the cessation from our works, and yet he has no delight in idleness and sloth, shows that the Sabbath was a ceremonial sign (see Exod[1] 31:13; Ezek 20:12), the substance of it is declared to be in Christ (Col 2:17; Heb 4:3). In other words, it signified the spiritual rest found

---

1. Calvin's *Commentaries* mistakenly cites the proof-text of *Ezek* 31:13 instead of *Exod* 31:13.

in Christ, when one ceases from his own works and is directed by the Spirit of God.

- The Lord does not forbid all works, since circumcision and sacrifices could be performed. But no works were allowed that could have been finished yesterday or postponed till tomorrow. Works of necessity (e.g., coming to the aid of one violently assaulted) and works of mercy (e.g., taking a fallen ox out of a pit) were allowable—the Sabbath was made for man, after all, not vice versa (Mark 2:27).
- The Sabbath's importance is noted by its being treated as a touchstone of religion (Jer 17:24; Ezek 20:21; 22:8; 23:38), and by the execution of a man who gathered wood on this day (Num 15:32).
- This commandment is not wholly ceremonial. An abiding feature is its objective to be a day of rest for considering the beauty, excellence, and fitness of God's works, both creative and providential.
- We must not rest merely at home but at the sanctuary with other believers, to pursue praying, sacrificing, and progressing in knowledge of the Law.
- It is also a day of rest for servants, but this is incidental to its main purpose of worship.
- God does not here command work for six days, but by way of contrast indicates his kindness by claiming only a seventh part of their time.
- That uncircumcised strangers were commanded to rest does not contradict the statement that the Sabbath was a sign between God and his people (Exod 31:13; Ezek 20:12). Their rest served no other purpose than that on this day no work should happen before the eyes of God's people, thus encouraging them to continue in restful obedience. This also may be seen from the demand for animals to rest.
- The reference to God's six days of creation probably indicates that Sabbath observance was prior to the giving of the Law. The Sabbath restriction with regard to the manna in the wilderness indicates this as well. Sabbath observance, however, became suppressed and nearly extinguished by men's depravity.

Exposition

Lev 19:30

You shall keep My Sabbaths and reverence My sanctuary: I am the Lord.

Lev 26:2

You shall keep My Sabbaths and reverence My sanctuary: I am the Lord.

Exod 23:12

Six days you shall do your work, and on the seventh day you shall rest, that your ox and your donkey may rest, and the son of your female servant and the stranger may be refreshed.

Lev 23:3

Six days shall work be done, but the seventh day is a Sabbath of solemn rest, a holy convocation. You shall do no work on it; it is the Sabbath of the Lord in all your dwellings.

Exod 31:12–17

And the Lord spoke to Moses, saying, ¹³"Speak also to the children of Israel, saying: 'Surely My Sabbaths you shall keep, for it is a sign between Me and you throughout your generations, that you may know that I am the Lord who sanctifies you. ¹⁴You shall keep the Sabbath, therefore, for it is holy to you. Everyone who profanes it shall surely be put to death; for whoever does any work on it, that person shall be cut off from among his people. ¹⁵Work shall be done for six days, but the seventh is the Sabbath of rest, holy to the Lord. Whoever does any work on the Sabbath day, he shall surely be put to death. ¹⁶Therefore the children of Israel shall keep the Sabbath, to observe the Sabbath throughout their generations as a perpetual covenant. ¹⁷It is a sign between Me and the children of Israel forever; for in six days the Lord made the heavens and the earth, and on the seventh day He rested and was refreshed.'"

Exod 34:21

Six days you shall work, but on the seventh day you shall rest; in plowing time and in harvest you shall rest.

Exod 35:1–3

Then Moses gathered all the congregation of the children of Israel together, and said to them, "These are the words which the Lord has commanded you to do: ²Work shall be done for six days, but the seventh day shall be a holy day for you, a Sabbath of rest to the Lord. Whoever does any work on it shall be put to death. ³You shall kindle no fire throughout your dwellings on the Sabbath day."

Lev 19:3

Keep My Sabbaths: I am the Lord your God.

- That Sabbath observance is linked to the tabernacle service shows that the rest from labor had reference to the sacrifices.
- The Sabbath was enforced with capital punishment since by its neglect religion would fall. This punishment, though, enforced the outward ceremonial rest, and so with the coming of Christ no longer applies.
- The prohibition of lighting fires included all food preparation and other normally allowable works. By noting an action so minimal, more involved actions were all the more forbidden.
- By "perpetual covenant" is meant the new state of things inaugurated by Christ's coming—the substance to which the shadowy Sabbath had been pointing. So though the external observation is now abrogated, its reality remains eternal (like circumcision).
- There was no time of the year or any conditions, even plowing and harvesting time, when Sabbath observance was not obligatory.

Fifth Commandment

*Honor your father and your mother,
that your days may be long upon the land
which the* L<small>ORD</small> *your God is giving you.*

General Principle: *Superiors must be gratefully revered and obeyed.*

Exod 20:12

Honor your father and your mother, that your days may be long upon the land which the Lord your God is giving you.

Deut 5:16

Honor your father and your mother, as the Lord your God has commanded you, that your days may be long, and that it may be well with you in the land which the Lord your God is giving you.

- God's Moral Law divides into two parts: first table is the first four commandments comprising piety; second table is the last six comprising charity towards other men.
- Human society cannot be maintained in integrity without children submitting to their parents and without other God-ordained authority figures reverently honored.
- Even natural reason discerns that the duties toward parents are: (a) reverence; (b) obedience; (c) an endeavor to repay what is owed to them, namely, grateful service.
- Even fathers unworthy of honor retain their right over their children, provided that honoring him does not detract from God's condemnation of his misbehavior.
- Obedience to parents is only "in the Lord" (Eph 6:1), which is to say that if they command any disobedience to God then obedience is freely to be denied them.
- God annexes the promises of a long and prosperous life. So though some disobedient children may have one (e.g., a long life), they will rarely have both (e.g., God repays them with disobedient children).

- By synecdoche, this law teaches that all lawful commands should obtain due reverence from us. God notes this via family relations because our pride resists submitting to the authoritative few, whereas most consider it gross barbarism to refuse honor to parents. God gradually moves from here to commands like "fear . . . the king" (Prov 24:21; cf. Rom 13:1; Eph 6:5; 1 Pet 2:13, 14, 18).

Exposition

LEV 19:3

Every one of you shall revere his mother and his father, . . .

- This commandment embraces obedience, and not merely reverence.
- God here shows how to honor parents, by exhorting children to beware of offending them.

POLITICAL SUPPLEMENTS

EXOD 21:15, 17

And he who strikes his father or his mother shall surely be put to death. . . . ¹⁷And he who curses his father or his mother shall surely be put to death.

LEV 20:9

For everyone who curses his father or his mother shall surely be put to death. He has cursed his father or his mother. His blood shall be upon him.

- Laying violent hands on parents or addressing them in abusive language merits the death penalty.
- Without such a penalty, a cruel barbaric society would result.
- Sinning against parents in any respect, or uttering a slight reproach against parents, as often happens in quarrels, does not come under this severe punishment.

DEUT 21:18–21

If a man has a stubborn and rebellious son who will not obey the voice of his father or the voice of his mother, and who, when they have chastened him, will not heed them, ¹⁹then his father and his mother shall take hold of him and bring him out to the elders of his city, to the gate of his city. ²⁰*And they shall say to the elders of his city, "This son of ours is stubborn and rebellious; he will not obey our voice; he is a glutton and a drunkard." *²¹*Then all the men of his city shall stone him to death with stones; so you shall put away the evil from among you, and all Israel shall hear and fear.*

- This law in a general way comprises the two previous laws.
- Those deserve to die that are of such a stubborn and intractable disposition as to reject parental authority and to hold them in contempt.
- By such laws we discover how we honor our parents.
- To prevent abuses, a legal trial ensued, whereby the parents brought the child before the local magistrates and presented their case. And though in this passage the punishment immediately follows the plaintiff's case, the child undoubtedly made his defense, and the judges, lest they be made non-entities at the trial, issued a verdict. For without a trial, any sort of injustice could happen: suppose the parents had a reputation for moroseness; the father could have accused the child by the instigation of a stepmother; some unworthy spite might be discovered; or the parents might have conspired to destroy their child in a fit of passion. A capital charge, moreover, makes a trial all the more necessary.
- Moses expressly mentions the vices of gluttony and drunkenness to show that though no capital crime was alleged [see Exod 21:15, 17; Lev 20:9], dissolute profligacy coupled with incorrigibility was sufficient for the penalty.
- The penalty's purpose is twofold: (a) to purge the earth of these sins that polluted it; (b) to deter similar crimes.

Exod 22:28

You shall not revile God, nor curse a ruler of your people.

Lev 19:32

You shall rise before the gray headed and honor the presence of an old man, and fear your God: I am the Lord.

Deut 16:18

You shall appoint judges and officers in all your gates, which the LORD your God gives you, according to your tribes, and they shall judge the people with just judgment.

Deut 20:9

And so it shall be, when the officers have finished speaking to the people, that they shall make captains of the armies to lead the people.

- These laws further explain, by synecdoche, that God includes all superiors in authority under the fifth commandment.

- Judges and magistrates should be thought and spoken about reverently. We must obey them not only from fear of punishment but "for conscience' sake" (Rom 13:5). And like parents, they should be revered even though they are not what they should be—not to excuse their faults but to deplore them silently rather than to subvert political government.

- Magistrates are figuratively called "gods" (Exod 22:28 can be translated "Thou shalt not revile the gods," as does the KJV). As ministers of God's authority, he has inscribed a mark of his glory upon them—even as fathers have been privileged with sharing God's title.

- Old men also have some sparks of God's glory thus requiring our honor. Even common sense dictates this, as pagans themselves recognize. And though some subvert their own dignity by wicked behavior, still according to God's command, age in itself is venerable.

- That God commands judges to be appointed in every city shows that their laws and edicts are to be obeyed—without which there could be no preservation and utility of society. The same holds true for military officers appointed during wartime.

Sixth Commandment

You shall not murder.

General Principle: *We must not vex, oppress, or hate anyone.*

Exod 20:13

You shall not murder.

Deut 5:17

You shall not murder.

- By synecdoche, all violence, smiting, and aggression are forbidden under the word "murder" (see Matt 5:22). God states the most extreme form of violence because everyone naturally finds murder abhorrent.
- Since in negative precepts the opposite affirmation also applies, here we are bidden not merely to abstain from wrongdoing, but to study how to love, defend, and hold dear our neighbor.
- This commandment extends to inward attitudes and intents (1 John 3:15).

Exposition

Lev 19:17

You shall not hate your brother in your heart.

- The Lord condemns even hatred in the heart, for the law is spiritual (Rom 7:14).
- This prohibition of hatred sufficiently proves that murder was forbidden.

Lev 19:18

You shall not take vengeance, nor bear any grudge against the children of your people, but you shall love your neighbor as yourself: I am the Lord.

- This commandment explains the sixth commandment as extending to inward emotions. We are commanded to love our neighbor, where also the opposite emotion of hatred is prohibited.
- God allows no malevolent or vengeful affections.
- Our Lord generally condemns this vice, though he expresses the prohibition as extending to the children of Abraham.
- To interpret it as commanding us to love ourselves first and then our neighbor is preposterous.

Lev 19:14

You shall not curse the deaf, nor put a stumbling block before the blind, but shall fear your God: I am the Lord.

- We must show special care to the weak and defenseless of our society, such as the blind and deaf, doing what we can to prevent their stumbling and falling.
- To insult the deaf is absurd and barbarous.

POLITICAL SUPPLEMENTS

Lev 24:17, 19–22

Whoever kills any man shall surely be put to death. . . . [19]If a man causes disfigurement of his neighbor, as he has done, so shall it be done to him—[20]fracture for fracture, eye for eye, tooth for tooth; as he has caused disfigurement of a man, so shall it be done to him. [21]And whoever kills an animal shall restore it; but whoever kills a man shall be put to death. [22]You shall have the same law for the stranger and for one from your own country; for I am the Lord your God.

Exod 21:12–14, 18–32

He who strikes a man so that he dies shall surely be put to death. [13]However, if he did not lie in wait, but God delivered him into his hand, then I will appoint for you a place where he may flee. [14]But if a man acts with premeditation against his neighbor, to kill him by treachery, you shall take him from My altar, that he may die. . . . [18]If men contend with each other, and one strikes the other with a stone or with his fist, and he does not die but is confined to his bed, [19]if he rises again and walks about outside with his staff, then he who struck him shall be acquitted. He shall only pay for the loss of his time, and shall provide for him to be thoroughly healed.

[20]And if a man beats his male or female servant with a rod, so that he dies under his hand, he shall surely be punished. [21]Notwithstanding, if he remains alive a day or two, he shall not be punished; for he is his property. [22]If men fight, and hurt a woman with child, so that she gives birth prematurely, yet no harm follows, he shall surely be punished accordingly as the woman's husband imposes on him; and he shall pay as the judges determine. [23]But if any harm follows, then you shall give life for life, [24]eye for eye, tooth for tooth, hand for hand, foot for foot, [25]burn for burn, wound for wound, stripe for stripe. [26]If a man strikes the eye of his male or female servant, and destroys it, he shall let him go free for the sake of his eye. [27]And if he knocks out the tooth of his male or female servant, he shall let him go free for the sake of his tooth. [28]If an ox gores a man or a woman to death, then the ox shall surely be stoned, and its flesh shall not be eaten; but the owner of the ox shall be acquitted. [29]But if the ox tended to thrust with its horn in times past, and it has been made known to his owner, and he has not kept it confined, so that it has killed a man or a woman, the ox shall be stoned and its owner also shall be put to death. [30]If there is imposed on him a sum of money, then he shall pay to redeem his life, whatever is imposed on him. [31]Whether it has gored a son or gored a daughter, according to this judgment it shall be done to him. [32]If the ox gores a male or female servant, he shall give to their master thirty shekels of silver, and the ox shall be stoned.

- To mutilate the body of another by blows was punishable.
- The Law of Retaliation (*Lex Talionis*) applied only to deliberate and premeditated acts, not accidents. The punishments equally fit the crime: life for life, tooth for tooth, and so forth.
- These laws were for both believers ("one from your own country") and unbelievers ("the stranger").
- Criminals should be torn even from God's altar, if to it they cleave, for it is disgraceful to abuse God's sacred name as affording license to sin.
- The light punishment of paying the victim's expenditures to recover was a concession to the hardheartedness of the Jews (see Matt 19:8), and as a chastisement to the weaker man (i.e., the victim) who rashly engaged in the conflict. Thus the political punish-

ment was not fully demanded by God, the stronger only paying the victim for his private loss.

- If a master struck his slave who then died immediately, the death penalty followed. If the slave lingered a day or two, there was no punishment, presumably because the correction was adequate, leaving no wounds or mutilation. God absolves none but he who only meant to chastise his slave. No punishment from the State followed because the loss of his money-maker was punishment enough.

- Abortion: To confine the death in Exodus 21:22–25 only to the mother is absurd, since the fetus even in the womb is a human being. It is a capital crime if the child or the mother or both die as a result of men recklessly fighting. If no death occurs, then the husband/father may sue for payment to compensate for the weakened status resulting from a premature birth.

- *Lex Talionis* was not applied when a master disfigured his slave. However, his status of superiority is forfeited (i.e., the slave goes out free) since he abused this status.

- To deter men from shedding blood, their animals that kill must be killed. If the master had knowledge of his animal's previous attacks, and through the master's negligence the animal attacks again and kills, the master must then be executed. The crime, though, is negligence, permitting judges to lessen the punishment to a fine.

- A negligent father in a similar situation, wherein his own children are killed by an animal, suffers a similar punishment.

- Negligence regarding the death of a slave was punished by killing the animal and fining the master.

DEUT 17:6

Whoever is deserving of death shall be put to death on the testimony of two or three witnesses; he shall not be put to death on the testimony of one witness.

DEUT 19:15

One witness shall not rise against a man concerning any iniquity or any sin that he commits; by the mouth of two or three witnesses the matter shall be established.

- The testimony of one witness was not enough to convict, but required two or three, hereby deterring rash accusations, light conjectures, insufficient accusations, and unjust prejudices.
- As from capital punishment we see how valuable the life of man is to God, so here we see God's care for the preservation of innocent blood.

Deut 22:8

When you build a new house, then you shall make a parapet for your roof, that you may not bring guilt of bloodshed on your household if anyone falls from it.

- Railings, or some enclosure, were required around roofs. As Israel's housetops were flat and company was there entertained, God took care lest incautiousness claim a life.
- Any loss of life "brings guilt of bloodshed on your household," requiring political punishment.

Deut 24:7

If a man is found kidnapping any of his brethren of the children of Israel, and mistreats him or sells him, then that kidnapper shall die; and you shall put away the evil from among you.

- The punishment of death was for kidnapping accompanied by selling into slavery. To deprive one of liberty deserves such a severe penalty.
- Since this crime would be immediately detected if sold in Israel, the sale would have to be in heathen nations, thus also separating the slave from the church.

Deut 21:22–23

If a man has committed a sin deserving of death, and he is put to death, and you hang him on a tree, ^{23}his body shall not remain overnight on the tree, but you shall surely bury him that day, so that you do not defile the land which the Lord *your God is giving you as an inheritance; for he who is hanged is accursed of God.*

- Wishing to ban inhumanity, God forbade a hanged body to remain overnight, requiring its burial that day. Otherwise it would "defile the land."
- Though those unworthy of a burial are in view here, the public good is regarded higher.

DEUT 25:1–3

If there is a dispute between men, and they come to court, that the judges may judge them, and they justify the righteous and condemn the wicked, ²then it shall be, if the wicked man deserves to be beaten, that the judge will cause him to lie down and be beaten in his presence, according to his guilt, with a certain number of blows. ³Forty blows he may give him and no more, lest he should exceed this and beat him with many blows above these, and your brother be humiliated in your sight.

- If anyone is judicially condemned to be beaten with stripes, the chastisement should not be excessive (viz., no more than forty stripes).
- God did not tolerate this to be performed by private individuals, but the criminal must be brought to the judges.
- The prohibition of excessiveness was either to prevent disfigurement, or to prevent ignominy and disgrace in the victim.

DEUT 24:16

Fathers shall not be put to death for their children, nor shall children be put to death for their fathers; a person shall be put to death for his own sin.

- God forbids the execution of children on account of their father's crimes. Such barbarism occurred at that time.

DEUT 20:10–18

When you go near a city to fight against it, then proclaim an offer of peace to it. ¹¹And it shall be that if they accept your offer of peace, and open to you, then all the people who are found in it shall be placed under tribute to you, and serve you. ¹²Now if the city will not make peace with you, but war against you, then you shall besiege it. ¹³And when the LORD your God delivers it into your hands, you shall strike every male in it with the edge of the sword. ¹⁴But the women, the little ones, the livestock, and all that is in the city, all its spoil, you shall plunder for yourself; and you shall eat the enemies' plunder which the Lord *your God gives you.* ¹⁵*Thus you shall do to all the cities which are very far from you, which are not of the cities of these nations.* ¹⁶*But of the cities of these peoples which the* Lord *your God gives you as an inheritance, you shall let nothing that breathes remain alive,* ¹⁷*but you shall utterly destroy them: the Hittite and the Amorite and the Canaanite and the Perizzite and the Hivite and the Jebusite, just as the* Lord *your God has commanded you,* ¹⁸*lest they teach you to do according to all their abominations which they have done for their gods, and you sin against the* Lord *your God.*

- Even in lawful war, God demands the repression of cruelty and minimization of bloodshed. Offers of peace are first necessary when coming upon a city. Capitulating cities then had tribute imposed upon them.
- God conceded to the hardness of the Jews' hearts in allowing them to kill the conquered males taken with arms and swords in hand. The perfect rule of justice, however, would not allow this.
- Conquerors must spare the women and children of the conquered cities.
- God distinguishes the common laws of war from those applicable to the Canaanite peoples. As God consecrated that land for his own service, he wished their race and memory to be wiped out from the land, lest the church be tempted to false superstitions.

Deut 23:15–16

You shall not give back to his master the slave who has escaped from his master to you. ¹⁶*He may dwell with you in your midst, in the place which he chooses within one of your gates, where it seems best to him; you shall not oppress him.*

- God allowed slaves that escaped from their masters to remain in Israel. They were not to be returned to their masters.
- To obviate the injustice of defrauding the master of his rightful property and money, and to prevent God's land from being a haven for evil, the slaves under consideration must be running from

excessive cruelty. No asylum for slaves running from the consequences of evil deeds is here envisioned.

- Judicial trials (inferable from the slave's choice of a city to dwell) justly uncovered the reason for the escape.

DEUT 22:6–7

If a bird's nest happens to be before you along the way, in any tree or on the ground, with young ones or eggs, with the mother sitting on the young or on the eggs, you shall not take the mother with the young; ⁷you shall surely let the mother go, and take the young for yourself, that it may be well with you and that you may prolong your days.

- We cannot kill an unhappy little bird who so endangers its life to be exposed to humanity so that it can be with its offspring. Also, that the preservation of the breed be regarded, the mother was allowed to go free.
- God provides here another instruction in the law of kindness. In this elementary lesson, God prohibited savageness and cruelty.

EXOD 23:5

If you see the donkey of one who hates you lying under its burden, and you would refrain from helping it, you shall surely help him with it.

DEUT 22:4

You shall not see your brother's donkey or his ox fall down along the road, and hide yourself from them; you shall surely help him lift them up again.

- The duties of humanity should be exercised toward brute animals that we may be more disposed to assist our brethren. God's main concern here is not for fallen oxen but for mankind (cf. 1 Cor 9:9).
- Believers would show forgiveness to their enemies by being merciful to their animals (Matt 5:44). We must conquer the ill will of our enemies by kindness.

NUM 35:9–34

Then the LORD spoke to Moses, saying, ¹⁰"Speak to the children of Israel, and say to them: 'When you cross the Jordan into the land of Canaan, ¹¹then you shall appoint cities to be cities of refuge for you, that the man-

slayer who kills any person accidentally may flee there. [12]They shall be cities of refuge for you from the avenger, that the manslayer may not die until he stands before the congregation in judgment. [13]And of the cities which you give, you shall have six cities of refuge. [14]You shall appoint three cities on this side of the Jordan, and three cities you shall appoint in the land of Canaan, which will be cities of refuge. [15]These six cities shall be for refuge for the children of Israel, for the stranger, and for the sojourner among them, that anyone who kills a person accidentally may flee there. [16]But if he strikes him with an iron implement, so that he dies, he is a murderer; the murderer shall surely be put to death. [17]And if he strikes him with a stone in the hand, by which one could die, and he does die, he is a murderer; the murderer shall surely be put to death. [18]Or if he strikes him with a wooden hand weapon, by which one could die, and he does die, he is a murderer; the murderer shall surely be put to death. [19]The avenger of blood himself shall put the murderer to death; when he meets him, he shall put him to death. [20]If he pushes him out of hatred or, while lying in wait, hurls something at him so that he dies, [21]or in enmity he strikes him with his hand so that he dies, the one who struck him shall surely be put to death. He is a murderer. The avenger of blood shall put the murderer to death when he meets him. [22]However, if he pushes him suddenly without enmity, or throws anything at him without lying in wait, [23]or uses a stone, by which a man could die, throwing it at him without seeing him, so that he dies, while he was not his enemy or seeking his harm, [24]then the congregation shall judge between the manslayer and the avenger of blood according to these judgments. [25]So the congregation shall deliver the manslayer from the hand of the avenger of blood, and the congregation shall return him to the city of refuge where he had fled, and he shall remain there until the death of the high priest who was anointed with the holy oil. [26]But if the manslayer at any time goes outside the limits of the city of refuge where he fled, [27]and the avenger of blood finds him outside the limits of his city of refuge, and the avenger of blood kills the manslayer, he shall not be guilty of blood, [28]because he should have remained in his city of refuge until the death of the high priest. But after the death of the high priest the manslayer may return to the land of his possession. [29]And these things shall be a statute of judgment to you throughout your generations in all your dwellings. [30]Whoever kills a person, the murderer shall be put to death on the testimony of witnesses; but one witness is not sufficient testimony against a person for the death *penalty.* ³¹*Moreover you shall take no ransom for the life of a murderer who is guilty of death, but he shall surely be put to death.* ³²*And you shall take no ransom for him who has fled to his city of refuge, that he may return to dwell in the land before the death of the priest.* ³³*So you shall not pollute the land where you are; for blood defiles the land, and no atonement can be made for the land, for the blood that is shed on it, except by the blood of him who shed it.* ³⁴*Therefore do not defile the land which you inhabit, in the midst of which I dwell; for I the* LORD *dwell among the children of Israel.'"*

DEUT 19:1–13

When the LORD *your God has cut off the nations whose land the* LORD *your God is giving you, and you dispossess them and dwell in their cities and in their houses,* ²*you shall separate three cities for yourself in the midst of your land which the* LORD *your God is giving you to possess.* ³*You shall prepare roads for yourself, and divide into three parts the territory of your land which the* LORD *your God is giving you to inherit, that any manslayer may flee there.* ⁴*And this is the case of the manslayer who flees there, that he may live: Whoever kills his neighbor unintentionally, not having hated him in time past—*⁵*as when a man goes to the woods with his neighbor to cut timber, and his hand swings a stroke with the ax to cut down the tree, and the head slips from the handle and strikes his neighbor so that he dies—he shall flee to one of these cities and live;* ⁶*lest the avenger of blood, while his anger is hot, pursue the manslayer and overtake him, because the way is long, and kill him, though he was not deserving of death, since he had not hated the victim in time past.* ⁷*Therefore I command you, saying, "You shall separate three cities for yourself."* ⁸*Now if the* LORD *your God enlarges your territory, as He swore to your fathers, and gives you the land which He promised to give to your fathers,* ⁹*and if you keep all these commandments and do them, which I command you today, to love the* LORD *your God and to walk always in His ways, then you shall add three more cities for yourself besides these three,* ¹⁰*lest innocent blood be shed in the midst of your land which the* LORD *your God is giving you as an inheritance, and thus guilt of bloodshed be upon you.* ¹¹*But if anyone hates his neighbor, lies in wait for him, rises against him and strikes him mortally, so that he dies, and he flees to one of these cities,* ¹²*then the elders of his city shall send and bring him from there, and deliver him over to the hand of the avenger of blood, that he may die.* ⁱ³*Your eye shall not pity him, but you shall put away the guilt of innocent blood from Israel, that it may go well with you.*

- The Lord instituted six cities of refuge to make a distinction between sins of malice and error, and to prevent the shedding of innocent blood. He that unintentionally and accidentally killed another might flee to one of these cities to escape the wrath of the victim's family.

- The cities were evenly dispersed throughout the land so that not too much traveling, and too much exposure to the avenger of blood, occurred.

- These cities were the portions of the Levites. In this way, the dignity of the Levites better protected the exiles. Their prudence and gravity were suited to shield the innocent but not the guilty.

- The intention, not necessarily the external act or the weapon (whether a mallet, stone, or sword), is what is relevant to discern if the act is criminal.

- Though punishments were to be inflicted by magistrates, and that only after due process, God here again concedes to the hardness of Jewish hearts: the avenger of blood could kill the killer under certain conditions. After a trial acquitted the innocent, they could be safe within the refuge city bounds. If, however, they exceeded the bounds, the avenger could exact revenge with impunity.

- After the death of the high priest, the innocent could then leave the city, thereafter any harm done by the avenger would have been criminal. With a new high priest, God's grace was then renewed, allowing the innocent freedom.

- A land stained with innocent blood is polluted and lies under God's curse until it is expiated by the murderer's execution.

Seventh Commandment

You shall not commit adultery.

General Principle: *We must not behave unchastely.*

Exod 20:14

You shall not commit adultery.

Deut 5:18

You shall not commit adultery.

- Chastity is generally exhorted in this commandment. Scripture uniformly commends marriage, while condemning sexual relations outside of it: Marriage is contrasted with whoremongers and adulterers (Heb 13:4). The daughters of Israel were forbidden from harlotry (Deut 23:17). "Harlotry, wine, and new wine enslave the heart" (Hos 4:11). Israel's corruptions were metaphorically called "fornications," being an inappropriate label if there was nothing wrong with it. Paul commands us not to commit fornication, reminding us of God's severe judgment upon Israel, killing twenty-three thousand (1 Cor 10:8), which judgment clearly reveals the unlawfulness of fornication. The Council of Jerusalem (see Acts 15) decreed fornication as forbidden, reasoning that "Moses [is] . . . read in the synagogues." Those who commit whoredom sin against their own body (1 Cor 6:18).

- By synecdoche, the broader term of *fornication* is comprehended under the term "adultery." Since the Law is the perfect rule of holy living, and fornication is everywhere condemned (see above proof-texts), then it is surely understood within the seventh commandment.

- God wills in us purity from all filthiness of the flesh and spirit (2 Cor 7:1) and to cherish modesty and chastity (1 Thess 4:4–5).

Exposition

LEV 18:20

Moreover you shall not lie carnally with your neighbor's wife, to defile yourself with her.

- While fornication pollutes a man, adultery violates the sanctity of marriage. It commingles seed, creating illegitimate offspring.

LEV 18:22–30

You shall not lie with a male as with a woman. It is an abomination. ^{23}Nor shall you mate with any animal, to defile yourself with it. Nor shall any woman stand before an animal to mate with it. It is perversion. ^{24}Do not defile yourselves with any of these things; for by all these the nations are defiled, which I am casting out before you. ^{25}For the land is defiled; therefore I visit the punishment of its iniquity upon it, and the land vomits out its inhabitants. ^{26}You shall therefore keep My statutes and My judgments, and shall not commit any of these abominations, either any of your own nation or any stranger who dwells among you ^{27}(for all these abominations the men of the land have done, who were before you, and thus the land is defiled), ^{28}lest the land vomit you out also when you defile it, as it vomited out the nations that were before you. ^{29}For whoever commits any of these abominations, the persons who commit them shall be cut off from among their people. ^{30}Therefore you shall keep My ordinance, so that you do not commit any of these abominable customs which were committed before you, and that you do not defile yourselves by them: I am the LORD your God.

- These verses discuss the behaviors of homosexuality and bestiality.
- It is a gross enormity for men endowed with reason to follow the behavior of non-rational beasts, who are satisfied with any natural connection. Such "perversion," as Moses calls it here, manifests a shamefully blind person (see Rom 1:28).
- These sins prevailed among the Gentiles surrounding Israel, therefore God warned his people of mimicking them. We also see that evil habits in no way excuse vice. He better deters them by forecasting his deadly judgment to be meted out on the Gentiles for these gross practices.

- God calls his people to walk in his precepts, statutes, and ordinances, being the light out of darkness. Because the Gentiles had not the Law, their behavior is not surprising.

DEUT 23:17

There shall be no ritual harlot of the daughters of Israel, or a perverted one of the sons of Israel.

- Here again fornication by women is prohibited.
- What is condemned in men is either fornication or male prostitution.

EXOD 21:7–11

And if a man sells his daughter to be a female slave ["maidservant," KJV], she shall not go out as the male slaves ["menservants," KJV] do. ⁸If she does not please her master, who has betrothed her to himself, then he shall let her be redeemed. He shall have no right to sell her to a foreign people, since he has dealt deceitfully with her. ⁹And if he has betrothed her to his son, he shall deal with her according to the custom of daughters. ¹⁰If he takes another wife, he shall not diminish her food, her clothing, and her marriage rights. ¹¹And if he does not do these three for her, then she shall go out free, without paying money.

- Here another vice was tolerated, the selling of daughters for the relief of poverty.
- If a man takes on a bondmaid intending to marry her, but then finding no pleasure in her decides not to marry, then he must allow her to be purchased from his care.
- If a man takes on a bondmaid to betroth to his son, he must provide her with a dowry ("deal with her according to the custom of daughters").
- If the son takes another wife in addition to the bondwoman betrothed to him by his father, the son could not diminish the bond wife's food, clothing, or appointed dowry. Otherwise she must be allowed to go free that her liberty may compensate for the wrong done to her.

- Even though the marriage covenant should remain inviolable (Matt 19:6), God made provision for rejected girls that they might not suffer infamy and injury.

DEUT 24:5

When a man has taken a new wife, he shall not go out to war or be charged with any business; he shall be free at home one year, and bring happiness to his wife whom he has taken.

- A newlywed husband is discharged from war duties in order to please his wife for one year. This prevents unfaithfulness in a couple who has not yet become thoroughly accustomed to each other.
- God has provided holy matrimony as a lawful avenue for our lusts. He, indeed, commands spouses to enjoy each other (1 Cor 7:3, 5).

NUM 5:11–31

And the LORD spoke to Moses, saying, ^{12}"Speak to the children of Israel, and say to them: 'If any man's wife goes astray and behaves unfaithfully toward him, ^{13}and a man lies with her carnally, and it is hidden from the eyes of her husband, and it is concealed that she has defiled herself, and there was no witness against her, nor was she caught— ^{14}if the spirit of jealousy comes upon him and he becomes jealous of his wife, who has defiled herself; or if the spirit of jealousy comes upon him and he becomes jealous of his wife, although she has not defiled herself—^{15}then the man shall bring his wife to the priest. He shall bring the offering required for her, one-tenth of an ephah of barley meal; he shall pour no oil on it and put no frankincense on it, because it is a grain offering of jealousy, an offering for remembering, for bringing iniquity to remembrance. ^{16}And the priest shall bring her near, and set her before the LORD. ^{17}The priest shall take holy water in an earthen vessel, and take some of the dust that is on the floor of the tabernacle and put it into the water. ^{18}Then the priest shall stand the woman before the LORD, uncover the woman's head, and put the offering for remembering in her hands, which is the grain offering of jealousy. And the priest shall have in his hand the bitter water that brings a curse. ^{19}And the priest shall put her under oath, and say to the woman, "If no man has lain with you, and if you have not gone astray to uncleanness while under your husband's authority, be free from this bitter water that brings a curse. ²⁰But if you have gone astray while under your husband's authority, and if you have defiled yourself and some man other than your husband has lain with you"—²¹then the priest shall put the woman under the oath of the curse, and he shall say to the woman—"the LORD make you a curse and an oath among your people, when the LORD makes your thigh rot and your belly swell; ²²and may this water that causes the curse go into your stomach, and make your belly swell and your thigh rot." Then the woman shall say, "Amen, so be it." ²³Then the priest shall write these curses in a book, and he shall scrape them off into the bitter water. ²⁴And he shall make the woman drink the bitter water that brings a curse, and the water that brings the curse shall enter her to become bitter. ²⁵Then the priest shall take the grain offering of jealousy from the woman's hand, shall wave the offering before the LORD, and bring it to the altar; ²⁶and the priest shall take a handful of the offering, as its memorial portion, burn it on the altar, and afterward make the woman drink the water. ²⁷When he has made her drink the water, then it shall be, if she has defiled herself and behaved unfaithfully toward her husband, that the water that brings a curse will enter her and become bitter, and her belly will swell, her thigh will rot, and the woman will become a curse among her people. ²⁸But if the woman has not defiled herself, and is clean, then she shall be free and may conceive children. ²⁹This is the law of jealousy, when a wife, while under her husband's authority, goes astray and defiles herself, ³⁰or when the spirit of jealousy comes upon a man, and he becomes jealous of his wife; then he shall stand the woman before the LORD, and the priest shall execute all this law upon her. ³¹Then the man shall be free from iniquity, but that woman shall bear her guilt.'"

- Causes of this ordeal: If a husband suspected his wife of unfaithfulness and could not otherwise be relieved from the anxiety (having no witnesses come forward), he could bring her before the priest at the tabernacle ("before the Lord"). The priest was to duly consider the matter before proceeding, as many men are insecure and causelessly suspicious. To offer husbands a blanket provision without leaving discretion to the priest would be like putting a sword into a madman's hands.

- Ordeal: The offering differed from ordinary offerings, containing no frankincense or oil, being a kind of solemn charge exposing her to the possibility of being cursed. She stood before God with head uncovered, while the priest filled an earthen vessel with holy water, threw dust from the ground into it, then also a writing of the curse. She was then to drink the water. This was all calculated to humble her that she not double her offense by perjury.

- Result: If the wife was guilty, her belly would swell and her thigh would rot. If she was innocent, she would be free and prolific.
- The concealing possibility of this crime called for such a rite.
- By this provision, God sought to capture adulterous women who thought they could escape by their cunning, and lest jealousy in the husband never depart from his mind causing dissension in the marriage. By this rite, therefore, God proclaims himself the guardian and avenger of conjugal fidelity.

Lev 18:19

Also you shall not approach a woman to uncover her nakedness as long as she is in her customary impurity.

- God here forbids husbands to sexually approach their wives during their monthly period. By this he intends to deter all filthiness, and to flourish chastity. For a couple to abandon themselves to so disgraceful an act, and rush headlong after their lusts, manifests that no modesty remains in them.
- Herein lays encouragement to husbands to enjoy their wife's embraces with delicacy and propriety.

Lev 18:1–4, 6–18

Then the Lord spoke to Moses, saying, ²"Speak to the children of Israel, and say to them: 'I am the Lord your God. ³According to the doings of the land of Egypt, where you dwelt, you shall not do; and according to the doings of the land of Canaan, where I am bringing you, you shall not do; nor shall you walk in their ordinances. ⁴You shall observe My judgments and keep My ordinances, to walk in them: I am the Lord your God. . . . ⁶None of you shall approach anyone who is near of kin to him, to uncover his nakedness: I am the Lord. ⁷The nakedness of your father or the nakedness of your mother you shall not uncover. She is your mother; you shall not uncover her nakedness. ⁸The nakedness of your father's wife you shall not uncover; it is your father's nakedness. ⁹The nakedness of your sister, the daughter of your father, or the daughter of your mother, whether born at home or elsewhere, their nakedness you shall not uncover. ¹⁰The nakedness of your son's daughter or your daughter's daughter, their nakedness you shall not uncover; for theirs is your own nakedness. ¹¹The nakedness of your father's wife's daughter, begotten by your father—she is your sister—you shall not uncover her nakedness. ¹²You shall not uncover the nakedness of your father's sister; she is near of kin to your father. ¹³You shall not uncover the nakedness of your mother's sister, for she is near of kin to your mother. ¹⁴You shall not uncover the nakedness of your father's brother. You shall not approach his wife; she is your aunt. ¹⁵You shall not uncover the nakedness of your daughter-in-law—she is your son's wife—you shall not uncover her nakedness. ¹⁶You shall not uncover the nakedness of your brother's wife; it is your brother's nakedness. ¹⁷You shall not uncover the nakedness of a woman and her daughter, nor shall you take her son's daughter or her daughter's daughter, to uncover her nakedness. They are near of kin to her. It is wickedness. ¹⁸Nor shall you take a woman as a rival to her sister, to uncover her nakedness while the other is alive."

DEUT 22:30

A man shall not take his father's wife, nor uncover his father's bed.

- God prefaces his prohibitions on sexual consanguinity by recalling the people to his statutes, which will lead them from the errors of their evil habits into the right way.

- The following marital and sexual relations God prohibits: (a) son and mother; (b) son-in-law and mother-in-law; (c) paternal or maternal uncle and niece; (d) grandfather and granddaughter; (e) brother and sister; (f) nephew and paternal or maternal aunt; (g) nephew and uncle's wife; (h) father-in-law and daughter-in-law; (i) brother-in-law and brother's wife; (j) step-father and step-daughter.

- Although there is no express prohibition against uncles marrying nieces, it must be unlawful because nephews are prohibited from marrying aunts (vv. 12–13). The reason for the nephew-aunt prohibition ("She is near of kin to your father or your mother") equally applies to the niece-uncle relation.

- A man may not marry a woman and her sister or any of her near kinsmen (even after the first wife's death). This prohibition is not so much to prevent incest but the cruelty of a husband.

DEUT 22:12

You shall make tassels on the four corners of the clothing with which you cover yourself.

- In order to further chastity, God commanded that flaps, drawn together by ties, be tied to gowns to cover the exposed thighs.
- This is a different law from that dealing with the reminder fringes sown onto garments to aid in recollecting the Law [see Num 15:37-41].

DEUT 22:5

A woman shall not wear anything that pertains to a man, nor shall a man put on a woman's garment, for all who do so are an abomination to the LORD your God.

- The Lord prohibits cross-dressing, lest women's modesty be hardened and lest men degenerate into effeminacy unworthy of their nature.
- Decency in the fashion of clothes is an excellent preservative of modesty.

POLITICAL SUPPLEMENTS

EXOD 22:19

Whoever lies with an animal shall surely be put to death.

LEV 20:13, 15–16

If a man lies with a male as he lies with a woman, both of them have committed an abomination. They shall surely be put to death. Their blood shall be upon them. . . . ¹⁵If a man mates with an animal, he shall surely be put to death, and you shall kill the animal. ¹⁶If a woman approaches any animal and mates with it, you shall kill the woman and the animal. They shall surely be put to death. Their blood is upon them.

- These are political enforcements of the moral prohibitions of Leviticus 18:22–30 (see above).
- That we may see how God abominates the crimes of homosexuality and bestiality, he prescribes execution as the penalty. In the case of bestiality, the beast must die as well.

Lev 19:29

Do not prostitute your daughter, to cause her to be a harlot, lest the land fall into harlotry, and the land become full of wickedness.

- God does not allow parents to prostitute their daughters. They rather should preserve their daughters by means of a pure and chaste education.
- "Lest the land fall into harlotry" declares this prostitution as criminal.

Lev 20:10

The man who commits adultery with another man's wife, he who commits adultery with his neighbor's wife, the adulterer and the adulteress, shall surely be put to death.

Deut 22:22–27

If a man is found lying with a woman married to a husband, then both of them shall die—the man that lay with the woman, and the woman; so you shall put away the evil from Israel. ²³If a young woman who is a virgin is betrothed to a husband, and a man finds her in the city and lies with her, ²⁴then you shall bring them both out to the gate of that city, and you shall stone them to death with stones, the young woman because she did not cry out in the city, and the man because he humbled his neighbor's wife; so you shall put away the evil from among you. ²⁵But if a man finds a betrothed young woman in the countryside, and the man forces her and lies with her, then only the man who lay with her shall die. ²⁶But you shall do nothing to the young woman; there is in the young woman no sin deserving of death, for just as when a man rises against his neighbor and kills him, even so is this matter. ²⁷For he found her in the countryside, and the betrothed young woman cried out, but there was no one to save her.

- God requires capital punishment for adultery. The marital covenant and conjugal faith should be held too sacred to be violated with impunity. Furthermore, it is an act of horrible perfidiousness to snatch from a man's bosom his wife who is his very life, or perhaps half of himself.
- It was not a capital offense for a husband to break faith with a single woman. Only with a wife is the crime, for the dishonor descends to the offspring, and the inheritance is transferred to strangers, and thus bastards unlawfully possess themselves of the family name.
- Even Gentiles have understood that the proper penalty for adultery is death. It is shameful for Christians not to at least imitate them on this point. The *pericope de adultera* [John 7:53—8:11] is wrongly appealed to by some, for Christ merely acknowledges that he is no judge, thus did not discharge the duties of a judge.
- A betrothed woman, counted as a wife, was considered a capital criminal who prostituted her virginity to another's embraces. If she was forcefully raped, however, and this can be satisfactorily proved by testimony and conjecture, then only the rapist must die.

Lev 19:20–22

Whoever lies carnally with a woman ["that is a bondmaid," KJV] who is betrothed to a man as a concubine, and who has not at all been redeemed nor given her freedom, for this there shall be scourging; but they shall not be put to death, because she was not free. ²¹And he shall bring his trespass offering to the Lord, to the door of the tabernacle of meeting, a ram as a trespass offering. ²²The priest shall make atonement for him with the ram of the trespass offering before the Lord for his sin which he has committed. And the sin which he has committed shall be forgiven him.

- Though in God's sight bond and free are equal, not so as regards the courts of justice. To lie with a betrothed bondmaid did not require death as with a betrothed free woman. Though worthy of death, on account of the people's hardheartedness the penalty was reduced to scourging of them both.
- An animal expiation was also required.

Exod 22:16–17

If a man entices a virgin who is not betrothed, and lies with her, he shall surely pay the bride-price for her to be his wife. [17]If her father utterly refuses to give her to him, he shall pay money according to the bride-price of virgins.

- Here God shows his care for young females, who, being deceived by a man, loses her virginity, with the seducer refusing to covenant with her.
- To prevent her despairing abandonment to prostitution (since she has lost her virginity), God requires the man to marry her. The man must also give her a dowry from his own property, lest if he should cast her off, she should not go away penniless.
- The father, however, can refuse her suitor while yet keeping the dowry.

Deut 22:13–21

If any man takes a wife, and goes in to her, and detests her, [14]and charges her with shameful conduct, and brings a bad name on her, and says, "I took this woman, and when I came to her I found she was not a virgin," [15]then the father and mother of the young woman shall take and bring out the evidence of the young woman's virginity to the elders of the city at the gate. [16]And the young woman's father shall say to the elders, "I gave my daughter to this man as wife, and he detests her. [17]Now he has charged her with shameful conduct, saying, 'I found your daughter was not a virgin,' and yet these are the evidences of my daughter's virginity." And they shall spread the cloth before the elders of the city. [18]Then the elders of that city shall take that man and punish him; [19]and they shall fine him one hundred shekels of silver and give them to the father of the young woman, because he has brought a bad name on a virgin of Israel. And she shall be his wife; he cannot divorce her all his days. [20]But if the thing is true, and evidences of virginity are not found for the young woman, [21]then they shall bring out the young woman to the door of her father's house, and the men of her city shall stone her to death with stones, because she has done a disgraceful thing in Israel, to play the harlot in her father's house. So you shall put away the evil from among you.

- God provides against unjust reproaches of husbands to their wives, and against a wife escaping punishment who had been defiled but pretended chastity.
- Parents, too, are admonished to be careful in watching over their children.
- It is an act of gross brutality that a husband who seeks divorce would willingly bring false charges upon his wife, reproaching her reputation.
- Once the legal charges have been brought, the parents could free their daughters from ignominy by producing her tokens of virginity.
- If the husband's charge is proved fraudulent, he is scourged, fined one hundred pieces of silver (which is given to the father), and forbidden to divorce her all his days—the opposite of the result he initially sought. If the wife is found guilty, she is executed for working wickedness in Israel, for abusing the sacred marriage institution, and for offering an unchaste body deceptively as a chaste one.

Deut 24:1–4

When a man takes a wife and marries her, and it happens that she finds no favor in his eyes because he has found some uncleanness in her, and he writes her a certificate of divorce, puts it in her hand, and sends her out of his house, ²when she has departed from his house, and goes and becomes another man's wife, ³if the latter husband detests her and writes her a certificate of divorce, puts it in her hand, and sends her out of his house, or if the latter husband dies who took her as his wife, ⁴then her former husband who divorced her must not take her back to be his wife after she has been defiled; for that is an abomination before the Lord, and you shall not bring sin on the land which the Lord your God is giving you as an inheritance.

- Although marriage is an inviolable institution, God here tolerates the unlawful practice of divorce due to the Jews' hardness of heart.
- This provision was given to women suffering cruelly under their husband.

- The bill of divorce cleared the woman of all disgrace, but cast some reproach upon the husband. He was thereby manifesting his fickleness, casting away his wife who was chaste but offended him by some other imperfection or disease.
- A man may not remarry his divorced ex-wife if she had an intervening marriage. To allow such would be to sanction his previous action of prostituting his wife. Since the liberty that he gave her could not abolish their marriage covenant, her subsequent marriage to another was adulterous (Matt 5:31; 19:9).

Lev 20:18

If a man lies with a woman during her sickness and uncovers her nakedness, he has exposed her flow, and she has uncovered the flow of her blood. Both of them shall be cut off from their people.

- This is the political enforcement of the moral prohibition of Leviticus 18:19 (see above).
- This severe punishment reveals the enormity of the crime in God's sight.

Lev 20:11–12, 14, 17, 19–24

The man who lies with his father's wife has uncovered his father's nakedness; both of them shall surely be put to death. Their blood shall be upon them. ¹²If a man lies with his daughter-in-law, both of them shall surely be put to death. They have committed perversion. Their blood shall be upon them. . . . ¹⁴If a man marries a woman and her mother, it is wickedness. They shall be burned with fire, both he and they, that there may be no wickedness among you. . . . ¹⁷If a man takes his sister, his father's daughter or his mother's daughter, and sees her nakedness and she sees his nakedness, it is a wicked thing. And they shall be cut off in the sight of their people. He has uncovered his sister's nakedness. He shall bear his guilt. . . . ¹⁹You shall not uncover the nakedness of your mother's sister nor of your father's sister, for that would uncover his near of kin. They shall bear their guilt. ²⁰If a man lies with his uncle's wife, he has uncovered his uncle's nakedness. They shall bear their sin; they shall die childless. ²¹If a man takes his brother's wife, it is an unclean thing. He has uncovered his brother's nakedness. They shall be childless. ²²You shall therefore keep all My statutes and all My judgments, and perform them, that the land where I am bringing you to dwell may not vomit you out. ²³*And you shall not walk in the statutes of the nation which I am casting out before you; for they commit all these things, and therefore I abhor them.* ²⁴*But I have said to you, "You shall inherit their land, and I will give it to you to possess, a land flowing with milk and honey." I am the* LORD *your God, who has separated you from the peoples.*

- Capital punishments apply to the following relationships (these politically enforce the previous moral prohibitions of Leviticus 18:1–4, 6–18): (a) step-mother and step-son; (b) father-in-law and daughter-in-law; (c) step-father and step-daughter; (d) a man and a woman with her mother; (e) brother and sister; (f) nephew and aunt; (g) a man and his uncle's or brother's wife; or any other similar incestuous relationship.
- Judges are not to give an empty show of clemency, but to exact God's precise justice. By "their blood shall be upon them," Moses shows that if judges do not place the guilt where it belongs then God's vengeance will be provoked against the whole community.
- God again directs Israel to his Law that lights the narrow way away from evil habits. He also reminds them that they inherit the Land on condition that they separate themselves from heathen nations.

DEUT 25:11–12

If two men fight together, and the wife of one draws near to rescue her husband from the hand of the one attacking him, and puts out her hand and seizes him by the genitals, ¹²*then you shall cut off her hand; your eye shall not pity her.*

- In the heat of a quarrel, when the agitation of the mind is ordinarily an excuse for excesses, it was a crime punished by cutting off her hand for a woman to grab the private parts of the man in the quarrel who was not her husband.
- This severe penalty shows how pleased is God with modesty.

Eighth Commandment

You shall not steal.

General Principle: *We must not unjustly gain from or defraud another.*

Exod 20:15

You shall not steal.

Deut 5:19

You shall not steal.

- Stealing involves secretly or violently taking the property of others, seeking gain from others' losses, accumulating wealth by unlawful practices, and being more devoted to our own private advantage than to equity.
- Since men cleverly name their vices as virtues, all fraudulent injustice is comprehended under the word *theft* so that all will abhor it as they naturally abhor thievery. God wipes away vain self-confidence by labeling such "virtuous" means of gain as theft.
- Positively, we are enjoined to safely care for our possessions, and that we promote our neighbor's advantage no less than our own.

Exposition

Lev 19:11, 13

You shall not steal, nor deal falsely, nor lie to one another. . . . ¹³You shall not cheat your neighbor, nor rob him. The wages of him who is hired shall not remain with you all night until morning.

- Theft includes all cases where deceit or violence is employed.
- An example Moses gives of fraud via unjust oppression is in the area of employer-employee relations. One breaks the eighth commandment if he sends away a worker without wages or defers his payment till tomorrow.

Deut 24:14–15

You shall not oppress a hired servant who is poor and needy, whether one of your brethren or one of the aliens who is in your land within your gates. ¹⁵Each day you shall give him his wages, and not let the sun go down on it, for he is poor and has set his heart on it; lest he cry out against you to the LORD, and it be sin to you.

DEUT 25:4

You shall not muzzle an ox while it treads out the grain.

- He who hires a poor person oppresses him if he does not give him immediate recompense for his labor, because the poor man sustains his life by his daily labors.

- God will visit the punishment upon violators of this law (Deut 24:14–15). This, therefore, is not to be politically enforced, and no legal suits can be brought.

- The righteous are noted by their compassion, even extending it to animals (Prov 12:10). And as oxen are to share in their own labors, all the more must men who labor be paid (1 Cor 9:10).

EXOD 22:21–24

You shall neither mistreat a stranger nor oppress him, for you were strangers in the land of Egypt. ²²You shall not afflict any widow or fatherless child. ²³If you afflict them in any way, and they cry at all to Me, I will surely hear their cry; ²⁴and My wrath will become hot, and I will kill you with the sword; your wives shall be widows, and your children fatherless.

LEV 19:33–34

And if a stranger dwells with you in your land, you shall not mistreat him. ³⁴The stranger who dwells among you shall be to you as one born among you, and you shall love him as yourself; for you were strangers in the land of Egypt: I am the LORD your God.

- We must cultivate equity toward all without exception. Even guests, sojourners, widows, and orphans in the land should be treated as if our own kindred.

- God personally threatens to exact vengeance on oppressors of the aforementioned, inasmuch as these are the defenseless and trampled-upon in society, having none to advise them. God will kill the oppressor and make his own wife a widow and his own children orphans, thus none should think they escape if earthly judges allow such oppression.

- God reminds Israel of their time as strangers in Egypt. They should remember the terror of oppression and understand the reasons that drive men to foreign lands (viz., poverty and hunger).
- That Israel was commanded to love strangers and foreigners as themselves shows that the name of *neighbor* extends to the whole human race, and not simply to our kindred or to those nearby (see Luke 10:30).

Deut 10:17–19

... God ... shows no partiality nor takes a bribe. ^{18}He administers justice for the fatherless and the widow, and loves the stranger, giving him food and clothing. ^{19}Therefore love the stranger, for you were strangers in the land of Egypt.

- By referencing his own nature, God declares that those among us of a vile and degraded position (i.e., widows, fatherless, strangers) receive his aid, inasmuch as he has no regard to persons. Christ also shows that a judgment is righteous that is not founded on appearance (John 7:23).
- God has respect unto the lowly (Ps 138:6), so that though no human aid may be found for them, divine aid and protection covers them.
- God proves his care for strangers by preserving and clothing them. To incite obedience to this law, the Lord again appeals to Israel's need for compassion while in Egypt.

Lev 19:35–36

You shall do no injustice in judgment, in measurement of length, weight, or volume. ^{36}You shall have honest scales, honest weights, an honest ephah, and an honest hin: I am the Lord your God, who brought you out of the land of Egypt.

Deut 25:13–16

You shall not have in your bag differing weights, a heavy and a light. ^{14}You shall not have in your house differing measures, a large and a small. ^{15}You shall have a perfect and just weight, a perfect and just measure, that your days may be lengthened in the land which the Lord your God is giving you. ^{16}For all who do such things, all who behave unrighteously, are an abomination to the Lord your God.

Eighth Commandment

- Commerce laws are here discussed, prohibiting deception in weights and measures (cf. Prov 20:10, 23).
- Moses enumerates some of the most injurious thefts, involving the grossest violation of public justice. They undermine all social rectitude, vitiate all contracts, and leave nothing in security.
- Though not civilly punishable, God summons men's consciences before his tribunal with threats and promises: honest business dealings prolong a man's life and corrupt business God finds abominable.
- God sets himself against all evil and illicit arts of gain.

DEUT 19:14

You shall not remove your neighbor's landmark, which the men of old have set, in your inheritance which you will inherit in the land that the LORD your God is giving you to possess.

- To secure everyone's property, landmarks set up for the division of fields should remain untouched as if sacred.
- They are thieves who unjustly possess another's land.

EXOD 22:26–27

If you ever take your neighbor's garment as a pledge, you shall return it to him before the sun goes down. ²⁷For that is his only covering, it is his garment for his skin. What will he sleep in? And it will be that when he cries to Me, I will hear, for I am gracious.

DEUT 24:6, 10–13, 17–18

No man shall take the lower or the upper millstone in pledge, for he takes one's living in pledge. . . . ¹⁰When you lend your brother anything, you shall not go into his house to get his pledge. ¹¹You shall stand outside, and the man to whom you lend shall bring the pledge out to you. ¹²And if the man is poor, you shall not keep his pledge overnight. ¹³You shall in any case return the pledge to him again when the sun goes down, that he may sleep in his own garment and bless you; and it shall be righteousness to you before the LORD your God. . . . ¹⁷You shall not pervert justice due the stranger or the fatherless, nor take a widow's garment as a pledge. ¹⁸But you shall remember that you were a slave in Egypt, and the LORD your God redeemed you from there; therefore I command you to do this thing.

- God here enforces a principle of equity with regard to loans: not to distress exceedingly the poor by too strictly requiring pledges.

- We cannot take anything in pledge necessary for the poor's subsistence—for example, depriving a farmer of his plough or a shoemaker of his workshop. To do so is to "take one's living."

- The Lord forbids creditors from ransacking the borrower's house in search of the appropriate pledge. The avaricious would seize upon all that was best, or would refuse all things thus filling the lowly with rebuke and shame.

- The creditor who refrains from taking a pledge most necessary to the borrower (e.g., bed, blanket, or garment) will receive God's blessing when the appreciative borrower prays for him. Therefore, money that may seem thrown away is divinely repaid. So we must remember that though the lowly have not the means to repay us in this world, still they have the power to do so before God. This implies the converse as well: that if the poor borrower should sleep inconveniently, or catch cold through our fault, God will hear and punish our cruelty.

- Such acts of kindness are accounted unto the man as righteousness. But such accounting is by God's gracious condescension unto believers. Only works that proceed from a pure and upright heart are righteous before God, and no such man can be found.

Exod 22:25

If you lend money to any of My people who are poor among you, you shall not be like a moneylender to him; you shall not charge him interest.

Lev 25:35–38

If one of your brethren becomes poor, and falls into poverty among you, then you shall help him, like a stranger or a sojourner, that he may live with you. ³⁶Take no usury or interest from him; but fear your God, that your brother may live with you. ³⁷You shall not lend him your money for usury, nor lend him your food at a profit. ³⁸I am the Lord your God, who brought you out of the land of Egypt, to give you the land of Canaan and to be your God.

Deut 23:19–20

You shall not charge interest to your brother—interest on money or food or anything that is lent out at interest. ²⁰To a foreigner you may charge interest, but to your brother you shall not charge interest, that the Lord your God may bless you in all to which you set your hand in the land which you are entering to possess.

- It is not enough to refrain from taking another's goods, but we must constantly exercise humanity and mercy in relief of the poor.
- The genuine trial of our charity is to lend expecting nothing in return. Since in lending, private advantage is sought, none but the rich would receive loans. But Christ obliges us to lend graciously so as not to exclude the poor (Luke 6:35).
- We must aid the poor in their necessities when afflicted with poverty—strangers and sojourners are included but especially those of the household of faith (Gal 6:10).
- A political law: They were prohibited from lending with interest to fellow Israelites who were poor (see Ezek 18:13), but could lend with interest to Gentiles. This was to equalize the treatment Jews were receiving in foreign lands. That this is a political law can be inferred from the distinction made between Jew and Gentile, a distinction the spiritual law does not admit. In the New Covenant, however, when the separator between Jew and Gentile has been removed, all men alike are to be free from interest and extortion.
- Yet not all usury is to be condemned without exception. Here are examples where interest can be justly charged: (a) To debtors falsely prolonging repayment to the loss and inconvenience of the creditor; (b) To a rich man who borrows money to buy a farm, who is charged by the lender part of the revenues of the farm until the principal is repaid.
- Usury and interest were only forbidden on the poor not the rich. All oppressive usury was also forbidden. This must be kept in mind when reading David's and Ezekiel's blanket prohibitions (Ps 15:5; Ezek 18:13).

- Now that Israel's political laws are abrogated (though the underlying principles of charity remain), only oppressive usury is now prohibited (i.e., that which contravenes equity and brotherly union).
- Crafty men might claim that since a commodity and not money was lent, then interest could be charged. But to circumvent all subterfuges, God prevents usury from being charged on anything lent.
- Since men desire wealth so strongly and greed blinds, God proclaims his blessing in opposition to all such iniquitous arts.

Deut 22:1–3

You shall not see your brother's ox or his sheep going astray, and hide yourself from them; you shall certainly bring them back to your brother. ²And if your brother is not near you, or if you do not know him, then you shall bring it to your own house, and it shall remain with you until your brother seeks it; then you shall restore it to him. ³You shall do the same with his donkey, and so shall you do with his garment; with any lost thing of your brother's, which he has lost and you have found, you shall do likewise; you must not hide yourself.

Exod 23:4

If you meet your enemy's ox or his donkey going astray, you shall surely bring it back to him again.

- We must study to do good, not simply refrain from doing evil. A disposition to aid our brethren is obliged, impelling us as far as our means and opportunities permit.
- In imitation of our Heavenly Father, we are obligated to assist even our enemies.
- If we find anything lost of our neighbor's, we must do what we can to restore it to its rightful owner.

Num 5:5–7

Then the Lord spoke to Moses, saying, ⁶"Speak to the children of Israel: 'When a man or woman commits any sin that men commit in unfaithfulness against the Lord, and that person is guilty, ⁷then he shall confess the sin which he has committed. He shall make restitution for his trespass in full, plus one-fifth of it, and give it to the one he has wronged.'"

- If anyone steals or fraudulently withholds something, they must make reparation.
- The sins considered secret are those not provable in a court of law. God bids those conscious of their fault to voluntarily restore what they wrongfully obtained.
- In addition to the property being restored, the penalty was 20 percent added to its value. This was not so much to enrich the victim (who would rather not have been violated in the first place), but to deter future crimes.

Exod 23:8

And you shall take no bribe, for a bribe blinds the discerning and perverts the words of the righteous.

Lev 19:15

You shall do no injustice in judgment. You shall not be partial to the poor, nor honor the person of the mighty. In righteousness you shall judge your neighbor.

Deut 16:19–20

You shall not pervert justice; you shall not show partiality, nor take a bribe, for a bribe blinds the eyes of the wise and twists the words of the righteous. [20] You shall follow what is altogether just, that you may live and inherit the land which the Lord *your God is giving you.*

- Moses forbids judges from accepting bribes. Receiving such gifts blinds the judge's eyes to justice and infects an otherwise sound mind.
- Since a judge's tribunal is, as it were, a sacred asylum to where the oppressed may fly, nothing more unseemly occurs than for it to fall among robbers. This evil is all the more egregious because their authority excludes all other remedies.
- The Lord places judging righteously in contrast to respecting the person.
- Since men's minds are so easily clouded by favor or hatred, and since God so wishes judges to study equity with inflexible constancy, he emphasizes just judgment by repetition: Deuteronomy 16:20 reads literally in the Hebrew, "That which is *justice, justice* shalt [judges] follow."

EXOD 23:3, 6

You shall not show partiality to a poor man in his dispute. . . . ⁶You shall not pervert the judgment of your poor in his dispute.

- Moses requires judges to judge matters justly, not taking into consideration a litigant's economic status—whether rich or poor.

- The poor are hereby protected lest their inferior social standing cause judges to deny them justice. The rich are hereby protected lest they be cheated by a litigious, audacious, and obstinate poor man.

POLITICAL SUPPLEMENTS

EXOD 22:1–4

If a man steals an ox or a sheep, and slaughters it or sells it, he shall restore five oxen for an ox and four sheep for a sheep. ²If the thief is found breaking in, and he is struck so that he dies, there shall be no guilt for his bloodshed. ³If the sun has risen on him, there shall be guilt for his bloodshed. He should make full restitution; if he has nothing, then he shall be sold for his theft. ⁴If the theft is certainly found alive in his hand, whether it is an ox or donkey or sheep, he shall restore double.

- Civil punishment for thievery: restitution of double the value if the merchandise is found; fourfold for sheep and fivefold for oxen if the merchandise had been killed or sold (because turning the theft into profit reveals greater obstinacy). The various fine amounts may be proportioned to the price of the article, the amount of harm caused, or the difficulty of the police investigation.

- The exception concerning the thief in the night (vv. 2–3a) is parenthetical to the overall passage. A man who kills a thief in the night is free from punishment because he could not see the behavior of the thief and because it is likely that a thief in the night will resort to violence since in the night he may only enter a house by violent damage. But if the thief is discovered in the day, when sunlight exposes the criminal, the killing is accounted murder and penalized by execution, for killing is too severe for theft.

- If thieves could not pay their fines, they were to be sold into slavery until it could be paid.

Exod 22:9

For any kind of trespass, whether it concerns an ox, a donkey, a sheep, or clothing, or for any kind of lost thing which another claims to be his, the cause of both parties shall come before the judges; and whomever the judges condemn shall pay double to his neighbor.

- The courts were made available to any who suspected another of stealing from him. Whoever lost the suit had to pay double the things lost. This wise remedy: (a) restored stolen property; (b) deterred thievery; (c) deterred false accusation; (d) cleared the name of those falsely accused.

Exod 22:5–8, 10–13

If a man causes a field or vineyard to be grazed, and lets loose his animal, and it feeds in another man's field, he shall make restitution from the best of his own field and the best of his own vineyard. ⁶If fire breaks out and catches in thorns, so that stacked grain, standing grain, or the field is consumed, he who kindled the fire shall surely make restitution. ⁷If a man delivers to his neighbor money or articles to keep, and it is stolen out of the man's house, if the thief is found, he shall pay double. ⁸If the thief is not found, then the master of the house shall be brought to the judges to see whether he has put his hand into his neighbor's goods. . . . ¹⁰If a man delivers to his neighbor a donkey, an ox, a sheep, or any animal to keep, and it dies, is hurt, or driven away, no one seeing it, ¹¹then an oath of the Lord *shall be between them both, that he has not put his hand into his neighbor's goods; and the owner of it shall accept that, and he shall not make it good. ¹²But if, in fact, it is stolen from him, he shall make restitution to the owner of it. ¹³If it is torn to pieces by a beast, then he shall bring it as evidence, and he shall not make good what was torn.*

- These passages address how controversies in things concealed should be concluded for the advancement of peace and equity.
- A man who, without permission, places his animal to eat in another man's field or vineyard shall restore double. The loss is to be made up at the highest estimate of its value (i.e., what it would have probably produced in its greatest state of fertility).
- A man who carelessly starts a fire that spreads to destroy another's property, the damage done must be repaid, even though no harm was intended.

- If a man deposits anything (e.g., garment, furniture) with his neighbor, and this neighbor alleges that it was stolen, if the thief is discovered then the thief must restore double. If the thief is not found, an oath shall be required of him who made the allegation. The oath is sufficient because we do not entrust anything to another unless we are persuaded of his honesty. If the deposit was an animal, and it has been violently carried away or torn by beasts, then the man was free who swears his innocence. But if it had been stolen then restitution was required from the depositary due to his negligence, for it is not easy to steal an animal from a stall or from a shepherd's hand.

EXOD 22:14–15

And if a man borrows anything from his neighbor, and it becomes injured or dies, the owner of it not being with it, he shall surely make it good. ¹⁵If its owner was with it, he shall not make it good; if it was hired, it came for its hire.

- These provisions concern *borrowing* property, not property deposited as in the previous provisions.
- If a lender witnesses the harm done to his property, then he shall bear his loss, provided no negligence or bad management is involved. But if harmed in his absence, the borrower must repay the loss.

LEV 24:18, 21

Whoever kills an animal shall make it good, animal for animal. . . . ²¹And whoever kills an animal shall restore it; but whoever kills a man shall be put to death.

- Whosoever inflicts a loss upon another, whether in a fit of passion or from unpremeditated impulse, he shall make an equitable satisfaction to the owner ("animal for animal").

EXOD 21:33–36

And if a man opens a pit, or if a man digs a pit and does not cover it, and an ox or a donkey falls in it, ³⁴the owner of the pit shall make it good; he shall give money to their owner, but the dead animal shall be his. ³⁵If one man's ox hurts another's, so that it dies, then they shall sell the live ox and divide the money from it; and the dead ox they shall also divide. ³⁶Or if it was known that the ox tended to thrust in time past, and its owner has not kept it confined, he shall surely pay ox for ox, and the dead animal shall be his own.

- Moses here considers more cases of damages inflicted requiring restitution.
- A man who opens a pit so that another's animal falls in and dies shall pay the owner of the animal for his loss. He is guilty of carelessness.
- Concerning one man's ox killing another's ox: (a) if done unexpectedly or by accident, then the live ox should be sold and the money divided evenly between the two parties; (b) if the ox was savage and had a reputation for such, the owner of the savage beast shall pay full value of the dead ox to its owner. The savage ox owner's carelessness gave occasion to the injury.

DEUT 23:24–25

When you come into your neighbor's vineyard, you may eat your fill of grapes at your pleasure, but you shall not put any in your container. ²⁵When you come into your neighbor's standing grain, you may pluck the heads with your hand, but you shall not use a sickle on your neighbor's standing grain.

- Out of care for the poor, God allows them to eat of another's field and vineyard for their fill and necessity.
- They can only eat what the need required, God forbidding that any should load up and carry away.
- This provision is also for travelers that they may not faint by the way when they become hungry (see Matt 12:1).
- Theft occurs whenever one breaks into another's field and gorges himself.

LEV 19:9–10

When you reap the harvest of your land, you shall not wholly reap the corners of your field, nor shall you gather the gleanings of your harvest. ¹⁰And you shall not glean your vineyard, nor shall you gather every grape of your vineyard; you shall leave them for the poor and the stranger: I am the LORD your God.

Lev 23:22

When you reap the harvest of your land, you shall not wholly reap the corners of your field when you reap, nor shall you gather any gleaning from your harvest. You shall leave them for the poor and for the stranger: I am the Lord your God.

Deut 24:19-22

When you reap your harvest in your field, and forget a sheaf in the field, you shall not go back to get it; it shall be for the stranger, the fatherless, and the widow, that the Lord your God may bless you in all the work of your hands. [20]When you beat your olive trees, you shall not go over the boughs again; it shall be for the stranger, the fatherless, and the widow. [21]When you gather the grapes of your vineyard, you shall not glean it afterward; it shall be for the stranger, the fatherless, and the widow. [22]And you shall remember that you were a slave in the land of Egypt; therefore I command you to do this thing.

- God inculcates liberality upon possessors of land when they gather their fruits. They may gather their produce while gratuitously leaving a portion for the poor to glean as their need required.
- Obedience to these laws brilliantly imitates God, who exercised his bounty before their own eyes by giving them much harvest.
- God did not require they give to the point of distressing themselves (2 Cor 8:13).

Deut 15:1-11

At the end of every seven years you shall grant a release of debts. [2]And this is the form of the release: Every creditor who has lent anything to his neighbor shall release it; he shall not require it of his neighbor or his brother, because it is called the Lord's release. [3]Of a foreigner you may require it; but you shall give up your claim to what is owed by your brother, [4]except when there may be no poor among you; for the Lord will greatly bless you in the land which the Lord your God is giving you to possess as an inheritance—[5]only if you carefully obey the voice of the Lord your God, to observe with care all these commandments which I command you today. [6]For the Lord your God will bless you just as He promised you; you shall lend to many nations, but you shall not borrow; you shall reign over many nations, but they shall not reign over you.

Eighth Commandment

⁷If there is among you a poor man of your brethren, within any of the gates in your land which the LORD your God is giving you, you shall not harden your heart nor shut your hand from your poor brother, ⁸but you shall open your hand wide to him and willingly lend him sufficient for his need, whatever he needs. ⁹Beware lest there be a wicked thought in your heart, saying, "The seventh year, the year of release, is at hand," and your eye be evil against your poor brother and you give him nothing, and he cry out to the LORD against you, and it become sin among you. ¹⁰You shall surely give to him, and your heart should not be grieved when you give to him, because for this thing the LORD your God will bless you in all your works and in all to which you put your hand. ¹¹For the poor will never cease from the land; therefore I command you, saying, "You shall open your hand wide to your brother, to your poor and your needy, in your land."

- Every seventh year the Jews were required to remit debts of their brothers.
- This law teaches that we should not be too rigid in exacting our debts, especially when it involves the needy.
- God also wished to restrain the tendency of the rich to oppress the poor. He wished to maintain in Israel a condition of mediocrity—not allowing a few rich people to tyrannize the general populace—thus preserving liberty.
- As the Sabbath was made for man, this seventh year Sabbath was a rest for the people as much as for the Land.
- Debts were not completely cancelled but only that their payments may cease for that year. God here bids his people to *lend* freely, which, if repayment became no longer required, would not be loans but gifts.
- God warns against stinginess with loans as the Sabbath year approached, promising to bless them who obeyed (cf. 2 Cor 9:6–11).
- Foreigners (i.e., unbelievers) could be sought after by creditors, as it would not be just for despisers of the Law to enjoy Sabbath benefits. God conferred these benefits on his elect people alone.

- Verses 4–5 are parenthetical, teaching that God presents us with an opportunity of doing good whenever any poor exists among our brethren. For this reason the Lord makes some rich and some poor, that by assisting each other he trains us up in the duties of charity [see Prov 22:2].
- God reminds his church that whatever they have results from his placement of them in his gracious covenant.

Exod 21:1–6

Now these are the judgments which you shall set before them: ²If you buy a Hebrew servant, he shall serve six years; and in the seventh he shall go out free and pay nothing. ³If he comes in by himself, he shall go out by himself; if he comes in married, then his wife shall go out with him. ⁴If his master has given him a wife, and she has borne him sons or daughters, the wife and her children shall be her master's, and he shall go out by himself. ⁵But if the servant plainly says, "I love my master, my wife, and my children; I will not go out free," ⁶then his master shall bring him to the judges. He shall also bring him to the door, or to the doorpost, and his master shall pierce his ear with an awl; and he shall serve him forever.

Deut 15:12–18

If your brother, a Hebrew man, or a Hebrew woman, is sold to you and serves you six years, then in the seventh year you shall let him go free from you. ¹³And when you send him away free from you, you shall not let him go away empty-handed; ¹⁴you shall supply him liberally from your flock, from your threshing floor, and from your winepress. From what the Lord has blessed you with, you shall give to him. ¹⁵You shall remember that you were a slave in the land of Egypt, and the Lord your God redeemed you; therefore I command you this thing today. ¹⁶And if it happens that he says to you, "I will not go away from you," because he loves you and your house, since he prospers with you, ¹⁷then you shall take an awl and thrust it through his ear to the door, and he shall be your servant forever. Also to your female servant you shall do likewise. ¹⁸It shall not seem hard to you when you send him away free from you; for he has been worth a double hired servant in serving you six years. Then the Lord your God will bless you in all that you do.

- God willed that his people should differ from heathen and ordinary slaves. Though these slaves had no limit, Hebrew slaves were to serve but six years.

- This exception applied: That if the slave married a slave woman and had children, his family should remain with the master, but he was free to go after the six years. By this we learn how hard was the condition of slavery, that a man might choose the unnatural break from his family instead of remaining in slavery. Since the slave woman was also the master's, and since the master had incurred expense in bringing up the children, the family stayed with him. This toleration of the severance of a marriage was on account of the Jews' hard hearts. But if the slave loved his master and family more than freedom he could give himself up to a perpetual slavery, that is, until the Jubilee Year.

- A public ceremony before the judges was performed for those choosing perpetual slavery. In this way, God deterred the secret tortures of masters who wished to compel the unwilling to continue as their slaves (see Jer 34:11). The ceremony involved boring through the slave's ear with an awl to a door or doorpost.

- When slaves were set free, God willed the masters to send them out liberally, with gifts from among their wine vats, their threshing floors, and their flocks. This was a moral law not to be civilly enforced. Not that the slaves were to be enriched, but the masters testified thereby of God's gracious bounty to them, and of the fact that it was by the slave's labors that their riches in part came, who served them twice as hard (or twice as long) as a hired servant.

Lev 25:39–55

And if one of your brethren who dwells by you becomes poor, and sells himself to you, you shall not compel him to serve as a slave. [40]As a hired servant and a sojourner he shall be with you, and shall serve you until the Year of Jubilee. [41]And then he shall depart from you—he and his children with him—and shall return to his own family. He shall return to the possession of his fathers. [42]For they are My servants, whom I brought out of the land of Egypt; they shall not be sold as slaves. [43]You shall not rule over him with rigor, but you shall fear your God. [44]And as for your male and female slaves whom you may have—from the nations that are around you, from them you may buy male and female slaves. [45]Moreover you may buy the children of the strangers who dwell among you, and their families who are with you, which they beget in your land; and they shall become your property. ⁴⁶And you may take them as an inheritance for your children after you, to inherit them as a possession; they shall be your permanent slaves. But regarding your brethren, the children of Israel, you shall not rule over one another with rigor. ⁴⁷Now if a sojourner or stranger close to you becomes rich, and one of your brethren who dwells by him becomes poor, and sells himself to the stranger or sojourner close to you, or to a member of the stranger's family, ⁴⁸after he is sold he may be redeemed again. One of his brothers may redeem him; ⁴⁹or his uncle or his uncle's son may redeem him; or anyone who is near of kin to him in his family may redeem him; or if he is able he may redeem himself. ⁵⁰Thus he shall reckon with him who bought him: The price of his release shall be according to the number of years, from the year that he was sold to him until the Year of Jubilee; it shall be according to the time of a hired servant for him. ⁵¹If there are still many years remaining, according to them he shall repay the price of his redemption from the money with which he was bought. ⁵²And if there remain but a few years until the Year of Jubilee, then he shall reckon with him, and according to his years he shall repay him the price of his redemption. ⁵³He shall be with him as a yearly hired servant, and he shall not rule with rigor over him in your sight. ⁵⁴And if he is not redeemed in these years, then he shall be released in the Year of Jubilee—he and his children with him. ⁵⁵For the children of Israel are servants to Me; they are My servants whom I brought out of the land of Egypt: I am the Lord *your God.*

- God, again inculcating humanity, commands his people to treat their slaves like hired servants, not harshly and contemptuously like captives. Envisioned here must be those who agreed to serve until the Year of Jubilee. Since these slaves were committed to longer periods of servitude, masters may be more inclined to treat them harshly, not fearing their near freedom.

- In the Year of Jubilee, Hebrew slaves were freed along with their wives and children.

- God claimed to have his property invaded should a man perpetually enslave one of his people. He had freed them from Egyptian slavery to be his own, and none should attempt to completely extinguish these marks of grace.

- Though this particular outward form of Moses' political law has been abrogated, the general principle remains: masters must not harshly treat their slaves, considering that their Heavenly Master watches them (Eph 6:9).
- Unbelieving foreigners and their children could be perpetually enslaved, as masters could leave to their own children the slaves as an inheritance.
- For those Jews who enslaved themselves to heathens in the Land, they could be redeemed by their relatives or by themselves should they obtain the sufficient funds (which were calculated according to the time from the Year of Jubilee). God willed that none of his children be alienated from the church and true worship of God. So though heathen masters were advantaged over Jewish masters in that their Jewish slaves served them until the fiftieth year while they served Jewish masters only until the seventh year, they were disadvantaged in that Jewish slaves could buy back their freedom at any time while this was not allowed when sold unto Jewish masters.

LEV 25:23–34

The land shall not be sold permanently, for the land is Mine; for you are strangers and sojourners with Me. ²⁴And in all the land of your possession you shall grant redemption of the land. ²⁵If one of your brethren becomes poor, and has sold some of his possession, and if his redeeming relative comes to redeem it, then he may redeem what his brother sold. ²⁶Or if the man has no one to redeem it, but he himself becomes able to redeem it, ²⁷then let him count the years since its sale, and restore the remainder to the man to whom he sold it, that he may return to his possession. ²⁸But if he is not able to have it restored to himself, then what was sold shall remain in the hand of him who bought it until the Year of Jubilee; and in the Jubilee it shall be released, and he shall return to his possession. ²⁹If a man sells a house in a walled city, then he may redeem it within a whole year after it is sold; within a full year he may redeem it. ³⁰But if it is not redeemed within the space of a full year, then the house in the walled city shall belong permanently to him who bought it, throughout his generations. It shall not be released in the Jubilee. ³¹However the houses of villages which have no wall around them shall be counted as the fields of the country. They may be redeemed, and they shall be released in the

Jubilee. ³²*Nevertheless the cities of the Levites, and the houses in the cities of their possession, the Levites may redeem at any time.* ³³*And if a man purchases a house from the Levites, then the house that was sold in the city of his possession shall be released in the Jubilee; for the houses in the cities of the Levites are their possession among the children of Israel.* ³⁴*But the field of the common-land of their cities may not be sold, for it is their perpetual possession.*

- As Israel's possession of the Land was a down payment and a symbol of God's salvific promise made to Abraham, God was unwilling that this inheritance should ever be lost.

- God here properly describes Israel's relation to the Land: He owned it, they were but tenants.

- The redemption of land could be by relatives of the seller or by the seller himself. If no redemption was made, the lands restored to their original owners in the Year of Jubilee. By this God wished to renew the marks of his original gracious bestowal of the Land.

- The Lord discusses the redemption of different kinds of houses. Houses sold *within* a city could be redeemed up to a year after the sell. If not redeemed, it should remain with the new owner even in the Jubilee. Houses sold *outside* a city, in a field, were treated the same as the lands in which they occupied, that is, they could be redeemed at any time or they returned to the original owner in the Jubilee. The rationale for this distinction: Houses in cites became burdensome and expensive. Selling them to the rich, therefore, was so the expenses could be maintained. Houses in fields were treated as the field because a field with no house was useless. Some place was needed to store the crop and to house the oxen.

- Levites could recover their sold city houses either by redemption or by the Jubilee. Otherwise, without a house in that area, temptations would arise to move to another area. But it was to the advantage of the people that the Levites remained dispersed throughout the Land. They were guardians of true religion, whereby God's blessings were enjoyed.

- The suburban fields of the Levitical cities—the lands where their cattle were supported—could not be sold. This, too, would have caused the Levites to move, thus ceasing to be strategically dispersed in the Land.

Deut 20:19–20

When you besiege a city for a long time, while making war against it to take it, you shall not destroy its trees by wielding an ax against them; if you can eat of them, do not cut them down to use in the siege, for the tree of the field is man's food. [20]Only the trees which you know are not trees for food you may destroy and cut down, to build siegeworks against the city that makes war with you, until it is subdued.

- Even during war, troops are to beware as much as possible of destroying the land that it not be too barren for future humanity. Militaries must spare fruit trees because they supply food to all men, but they may use non-food trees for ramparts, bulwarks, and other battle helps.
- This is not a strict rule. If necessity demands, they may even use fruit trees.

Deut 21:14–17

And it shall be, if you have no delight in her, then you shall set her free, but you certainly shall not sell her for money; you shall not treat her brutally, because you have humbled her. [15]If a man has two wives, one loved and the other unloved, and they have borne him children, both the loved and the unloved, and if the firstborn son is of her who is unloved, [16]then it shall be, on the day he bequeaths his possessions to his sons, that he must not bestow firstborn status on the son of the loved wife in preference to the son of the unloved, the true firstborn. [17]But he shall acknowledge the son of the unloved wife as the firstborn by giving him a double portion of all that he has, for he is the beginning of his strength; the right of the firstborn is his.

- If a man dishonors a captive woman by refusing to marry her after having taken her for this purpose, he could not sell her but had to free her. In this way he somewhat diminished her injury. So though he was impelled by his lust to a rash decision, the penalty of lust was that this conqueror should lose his plunder.
- To prevent the defrauding of rights, God forbids a polygamist from transferring the firstborn rights to the child of his second wife, whom he loves more than his first wife. A man who arrogates such power to himself almost claims the ability to create.

Deut 20:5–8

Then the officers shall speak to the people, saying: "What man is there who has built a new house and has not dedicated it? Let him go and return to his house, lest he die in the battle and another man dedicate it. ⁶Also what man is there who has planted a vineyard and has not eaten of it? Let him go and return to his house, lest he die in the battle and another man eat of it. ⁷And what man is there who is betrothed to a woman and has not married her? Let him go and return to his house, lest he die in the battle and another man marry her." ⁸The officers shall speak further to the people, and say, "What man is there who is fearful and fainthearted? Let him go and return to his house, lest the heart of his brethren faint like his heart."

- As it is beneficial to the State that vineyards are planted, houses are built, and people marry, and as these are not sufficiently undertaken if men believe they have little hope of enjoying them, God provides exemption from battle for those who have newly undertaken these endeavors.
- As it concerns the whole people to have soldiers ready for war, God provides exemptions for the fearful soldier.
- Regarding marriage, if the husband be deprived of leaving progeny, inheritance rights might be transferred to another.
- God shows the justice of us peaceably enjoying our possessions, that he requires such indulgences during war. How much more intolerable is it if men are driven from their possessions during peace!

Deut 25:5–10

If brothers dwell together, and one of them dies and has no son, the widow of the dead man shall not be married to a stranger outside the family; her husband's brother shall go in to her, take her as his wife, and perform the duty of a husband's brother to her. ⁶And it shall be that the firstborn son which she bears will succeed to the name of his dead brother, that his name may not be blotted out of Israel. ⁷But if the man does not want to take his brother's wife, then let his brother's wife go up to the gate to the elders, and say, "My husband's brother refuses to raise up a name to his brother in Israel; he will not perform the duty of my husband's brother." ⁸Then the elders of his city shall call him and speak to him. But if he stands firm and says, "I do not want to take her," ⁹then his brother's wife shall come to him in the presence of the elders, remove his sandal from his foot, spit in his face, and answer and say, "So shall it be done to the man who will not build up his brother's house." ¹⁰And his name shall be called in Israel, "The house of him who had his sandal removed."

- Here again, God wishes to preserve to every man, even the dead, what he possesses.

- If a man died leaving no child, a near relative of his was to marry his widow and raise up to her a child. In this way, the dead man's name might not become extinct.

- The relative in view is not a brother, for this was forbidden. More distant relatives are meant.

- It was considered a kind of theft for a near kinsman to refuse to obviate the dead man's childlessness. By a public ceremony before the elders of the city, such a relative renounced his right to the relationship and any advantages from it.

- The trial was also to acquire for the widow the liberty to marry into another family, should there be no near relative able or willing to take on the task.

Ninth Commandment

You shall not bear false witness against your neighbor.

General Principle: *We must not allow our neighbors to be defamed.*

Exod 20:16

You shall not bear false witness against your neighbor.

Deut 5:20

You shall not bear false witness against your neighbor.

- As God has shown care to protect people's fortunes, it would be absurd if he did not also protect their reputations, which is more precious.
- God condemns falsehoods purposing to injure the innocent, whether in court by public testimony, or in the streets, or in private houses, or secret corners.
- What is affirmed: to have kind, equitable, and pure interpretations of our neighbor's acts and words. We must not burden them with false reproaches.
- What is forbidden: (a) to become complicit in, or to listen eagerly to, the circulation of reproaches or sinister reports in hatred (Prov 10:12)—even if the reports may be true, if it proceeds from an outburst of anger or ill will, we condemn ourselves; (b) all hateful language tending to bring disgrace on our brethren; (c) all bold and disrespectful talk whereby our brother's good name suffers injury; (d) all detractions that flow from malice, envy, rivalry, or any other improper feelings, for we must not be too suspicious or too curious in observing the defects of others.

Exposition

EXOD 23:1–2, 7

You shall not circulate a false report. Do not put your hand with the wicked to be an unrighteous witness. ²You shall not follow a crowd to do evil; nor shall you testify in a dispute so as to turn aside after many to pervert justice. . . . ⁷Keep yourself far from a false matter; do not kill the innocent and righteous. For I will not justify the wicked.

LEV 19:16–17

You shall not go about as a talebearer among your people; nor shall you take a stand against the life of your neighbor: I am the LORD. . . . ¹⁷You shall surely rebuke your neighbor, and not bear sin because of him.

- We cannot receive a false report of our neighbor and pass it on.
- None should willingly give way to the unjust opinions of the masses. Otherwise, we keep lies alive that would die of their own emptiness.
- Perjury is here condemned that brings about the death of the innocent. God calls such perjurers before his judgment seat that they may know this act will be punished.
- Moses designates as vagabonds those who eagerly run to and fro bringing quiet people into trouble, and who, in their malignant inquisitiveness, penetrate into everyone's secrets.
- Such vagabonds should be rebuked privately not publicly. To publicly denounce him partakes in his infamy and precipitates his ruin. A well-regulated zeal consults the welfare of the one who is ruining himself (Matt 18:15).

POLITICAL SUPPLEMENTS

DEUT 19:16–21

If a false witness rises against any man to testify against him of wrongdoing, ¹⁷then both men in the controversy shall stand before the LORD, before the priests and the judges who serve in those days. ¹⁸And the judges shall make careful inquiry, and indeed, if the witness is a false witness, who has testified falsely against his brother, ¹⁹then you shall do to him as he thought to have done to his brother; so you shall put away the evil from among you. ²⁰And those who remain shall hear and fear, and hereafter they shall not again commit such evil among you. ²¹Your eye shall not pity: life shall be for life, eye for eye, tooth for tooth, hand for hand, foot for foot.

- The political punishment for perjury was the Law of Retaliation ("eye for an eye").
- Moses requires judges to examine diligently the charges before issuing any verdict.

Tenth Commandment

*You shall not covet your neighbor's house;
you shall not covet your neighbor's wife,
nor his male servant, nor his female servant,
nor his ox, nor his donkey,
nor anything that is your neighbor's.*

General Principle: *We must not be (internally) disposed to sin.*

Exod 20:17

You shall not covet your neighbor's house; you shall not covet your neighbor's wife, nor his male servant, nor his female servant, nor his ox, nor his donkey, nor anything that is your neighbor's.

Deut 5:21

You shall not covet your neighbor's wife; and you shall not desire your neighbor's house, his field, his male servant, his female servant, his ox, his donkey, or anything that is your neighbor's.

- This commandment extends to the preceding nine commandments. Those not only applied to external acts but also to the inner desires of the heart—secret unchastity, unlawful appetites for gain, and so forth. "You shall not covet," then, was given that none might escape the inner requirements of the laws, an escape that might have seemed plausible if one simply paid attention to the wording of the laws. So, like Paul, this commandment awakens our mind to the depth of the Law (Rom 7:7, 14).
- God here ascends to the fountain of all sins.
- Corrupt thoughts that arise spontaneously and then vanish are not in view. Sin arises only when they affect us pleasantly.

Sum and Use of the Law

SUM OF THE LAW

DEUT 10:12–13

And now, Israel, what does the LORD your God require of you, but to fear the LORD your God, to walk in all His ways and to love Him, to serve the LORD your God with all your heart and with all your soul, ¹³and to keep the commandments of the LORD and His statutes which I command you today for your good?

DEUT 6:5

You shall love the LORD your God with all your heart, with all your soul, and with all your strength.

LEV 19:18

You shall love your neighbor as yourself: . . .

- Paul teaches that the Law's purpose "is love from a pure heart, from a good conscience, and from sincere faith" (1 Tim 1:5), and that those teachers who had swerved from that end had "turned aside to idle talk" [1 Tim 1:6].
- Moses sums up all of our duties under two heads: piety and justice. As Christ, the inspiration of Moses, also taught: all the Law is to love God together with our neighbors (Matt 22:37).
- Loving our neighbor is proof that we love God (1 John 4:20–21). In this way religious hypocrites are exposed, who cover themselves with ceremonies yet inwardly and outwardly sin against their neighbor. Moreover, when the New Testament comprises all the Law under loving our neighbor (Matt 19:18; Gal 5:14; Rom 13:8), it presupposes the love of God.
- Moses tells us that the fear and love of God are the motives by which the Law is kept.

- As self-love blinds us, God wills us to direct that love to others, for love "does not seek its own" (1 Cor 13:5). And "neighbor" includes not merely our close connections but all without exception (Lev 19:33–34; Luke 10:30).

USE OF THE LAW

1. *Moral use*: regulates our living so that we not wander through life in uncertainty.
2. *Theological use*: convicts men of their iniquity, that they might acknowledge themselves to be lost, and may learn to fly to God's mercy in Christ for refuge.

When the New Testament seemingly disparages the Law it is either:

> (a) Correcting those who advocated a *misuse* of the Law by teaching justification by works of the law (see 2 Cor 3:6)—such an error seeks to trample the Gospel. In substance, the teachings of Moses and Christ perfectly accord.
>
> or:
>
> (b) Abrogating the use of Old Covenant ceremonies.

Bibliography

Bahnsen, Greg L. *By This Standard: The Authority of God's Law Today*. Tyler, TX: Institute for Christian Economics, 1985.
———. *Homosexuality: A Biblical View*. Phillipsburg, NJ: P & R, 1978.
———. *Van Til's Apologetic: Readings and Analysis*. Phillipsburg, NJ: P & R, 1998.
Budziszewski, J. Review of *Homosexuality and American Public Life*, edited by Christopher Wolfe. *Catholic Education Resource Center*. Online: http://www.catholiceducation.org/ articles/homosexuality/ho0057.html (accessed August 12, 2008).
———. "The Natural Law Is What We Naturally Know." *Acton Institute*. Online: http://www.acton.org/publications/randl/rl_interview_460.php (accessed August 8, 2008).
———. *Written on the Heart: The Case for Natural Law*. Downers Grove, IL: InterVarsity, 1997.
Calvin, John. *Commentaries on the Four Last Books of Moses Arranged in the Form of a Harmony*. Translated by Rev. Charles William Bingham. Edinburgh, Scotland: Calvin Translation Society, 1843. Reprint, Grand Rapids, MI: Baker, 2003.
———. *Commentary on the Gospel According to John*. Translated by Rev. William Pringle. Edinburgh, Scotland: Calvin Translation Society, 1843. Reprint, Grand Rapids, MI: Baker, 2003.
———. *Commentary upon the Acts of the Apostles*. Vol. 1. Edited by Henry Beveridge. Translated by Christopher Fetherstone. Edinburgh, Scotland: Calvin Translation Society, 1843. Reprint, Grand Rapids, MI: Baker, 2003.
———. *Commentaries on the Epistle of Paul the Apostle to the Romans*. Translated and edited by Rev. John Owen. Edinburgh, Scotland: Calvin Translation Society, 1843. Reprint, Grand Rapids, MI: Baker, 2003.
———. *Commentary on the Epistles of Paul the Apostle to the Corinthians*. Translated by Rev. John Pringle. Edinburgh, Scotland: Calvin Translation Society, 1843. Reprint, Grand Rapids, MI: Baker, 2003.
———. *Commentaries on the Epistles to Timothy, Titus, and Philemon*. Translated by Rev. William Pringle. Edinburgh, Scotland: Calvin Translation Society, 1843. Reprint, Grand Rapids, MI: Baker, 2003.
———. *Commentaries on the Epistle of Paul the Apostle to the Hebrews*. Translated and edited by Rev. John Owen. Edinburgh, Scotland: Calvin Translation Society, 1843. Reprint, Grand Rapids, MI: Baker, 1999.
———. *Calvin: Institutes of the Christian Religion*. Vols. 20 and 21 of *The Library of Christian Classics*. Edited by John T. McNeill. Translated by Ford Lewis Battles. Philadelphia: Westminster, 1960.
———. "Adultery and Its Penalty." *Calvin Speaks* 2, no. 4 (April 1981). Edited by James B. Jordan. Online: http://www.garynorth.com/freebooks/docs/a_pdfs/newslet/calvin/8104.PDF (accessed January 19, 2009).

———. *The Covenant Enforced: Sermons on Deuteronomy 27 and 28*. Edited by James B. Jordan. Tyler, TX: Institute for Christian Economics, 1990.

Catechism of the Catholic Church. 2d Ed. Paragraph 2366. Online: http://www.scborromeo.org/ccc/p3s2c2a6.htm#III (accessed December 29, 2009).

Clouser, Roy. *The Myth of Religious Neutrality*. Notre Dame: University of Notre Dame Press, 1991.

Fisher, George Park. *History of the Christian Church*. Nashville: Charles Scribner's Sons, 1887.

Frame, John. *The Doctrine of the Christian Life*. A Theology of Lordship. Phillipsburg, NJ: P & R, 2008.

———. "Is Natural Revelation Sufficient to Govern Culture?" The Works of John Frame and Vern Poythress. Online: http://www.frame-poythress.org/frame_articles/2006Natural Revelation.htm (accessed June 29, 2008).

God's Law in Modern Times: A Debate: P. Andrew Sandlin vs. Prof. David VanDrunen. Available from *Covenant Media Foundation*. CD. http://www.cmfnow.com/godslawin moderntimesadebate.aspx.

Gordon, T. David. "The Insufficiency of Scripture." Online: http://www.covopc.org/Papers/ Insufficiency _of_Scripture.html (accessed August 8, 2008).

Grudem, Wayne. *Politics—According to the Bible: A Comprehensive Resource for Understanding Modern Political Issues in Light of Scripture*. Grand Rapids, MI: Zondervan, 2010.

Gundry, Stanley N., ed. *Five Views on Law and Gospel*. Counterpoints. Grand Rapids, MI: Zondervan, 1996.

Irons, Lee. "What I Believe About Homosexuality." The Upper Register. Online: http://www.upperregister.com/irons_trial/WhatIBelieveAboutHomosexuality(Irons).pdf (accessed December 18, 2009).

Kurtz, Paul. *Living Without Religion: Eupraxophy*. Amherst, NY: Prometheus, 1994.

Meacham, Jon. "The End of Christian America." *Newsweek*, April 13, 2009. Online: http://www.newsweek.com/id/192583 (accessed April 8, 2009).

Morey, Robert A. *How the Old and New Testaments Relate to Each Other*. Las Vegas: Christian Scholars, 2002.

Murray, John. *Principles of Conduct: Aspects of Biblical Ethics*. Grand Rapids, MI: Eerdmans, 1957.

———. *Collected Writings of John Murray*. Vol. 1: The Claims of Truth. Carlisle, PA: Banner of Truth Trust, 1976.

The New Encyclopedia Britannica. 15th ed. Edited by Philip W. Goetz. Vol. 15. Chicago: Encyclopedia Britannica, 1991.

Ryrie, Charles C. *Dispensationalism*. Rev. and exp. ed. Chicago: Moody, 2007.

Symington, William. *Messiah the Prince or, The Mediatorial Dominion of Jesus Christ*. National Reform Association, 1884. Reprint, Pittsburgh: Christian Statesman, 1999.

VanDrunen, David. *A Biblical Case for Natural Law*. Studies in Christian Social Ethics and Economics, Number 1. Edited by Anthony B. Bradley. Grand Rapids, MI: Acton Institute, n.d.

———. "Natural Law and Christians in the Public Square." *Modern Reformation*. Online: http://www.modernreformation.org/default.php?page=articledisplay&var1=ArtRead&var2=93&var3=authorbio&var4=AutRes&var5=62 (accessed January 6, 2009).

———. "VanDrunen in the Hands of an Anxious Kloosterman: A Response to a Review of a Biblical Case for Natural Law." *Ordained Servant Online.* Online: http://www.opc.org/os.html?article_id=78 (accessed August 16, 2008).

Van Til, Cornelius. *Common Grace and the Gospel.* Phillipsburg, NJ: P & R, 1972.

Scripture Index A

Calvin's Expositional Order

(Designed for Calvin scholars, this index is the Scripture order Calvin presents in his commentaries.)

PREFACE

Exod 20:1–2	2
Deut 5:1–6	2
Deut 4:20	2
Lev 19:36–37	3
Lev 20:8	3
Lev 22:31–33	3
Deut 4:1–2	3
Deut 5:32–33	3
Deut 13:18	3
Deut 4:5–14	4
Deut 4:32–40	5
Deut 7:6–8	6
Deut 10:14–17	6
Deut 27:9–10	6
Deut 26:16–19	7
Deut 6:20–25	7
Num 15:37–41	8
Deut 6:6–9	8
Deut 11:18–20	8
Exod 23:13	8
Deut 27:1–4, 8	9
Deut 31:10–13	9
Deut 6:10–12	10
Deut 9:1–6	10
Deut 10:21–22	11
Deut 11:1–7	11
Deut 8:1–6	12
Deut 11:8–9	12
Deut 29:2–9	12
Deut 8:7–10	13
Deut 11:10–12	13
Deut 6:1–3, 17–19	14
Deut 8:11–18	14
Exod 23:20–23, 25–31	15
Deut 29:29	16
Deut 30:11–14	16
Lev 27:34	17
Deut 1:1–5	17
Deut 4:44–49	17
Deut 29:1	17

FIRST

Exod 20:3	20
Deut 5:7	20
Deut 6:4, 13	20
Deut 10:20	20
Deut 6:16	20
Lev 19:1–2	21
Deut 6:14–15	21
Deut 18:9–14	21
Deut 18:15–18	22
Deut 13:1–4	23
Deut 18:21–22	23
Lev 18:21	23
Lev 19:26, 31	24
Deut 12:29–32	24
Deut 18:19	24

Scripture Index A

Deut 13:5	24	Deut 17:2–5, 7	46
Deut 17:12–13	25		
Deut 13:6–11	26	**THIRD**	
Deut 13:12–17	27		
Exod 22:18	28	Exod 20:7	50
Lev 20:6, 27	28	Deut 5:11	50
Num 15:30–31	28	Lev 19:12	50
Lev 20:1–5	28	Exod 23:13	51
Exod 12:15, 19	28	Deut 6:13	51
Deut 17:14–20	29	Deut 10:20	51
Deut 20:1–4	30	Deut 23:21–23	51
Num 10:1–10	31	Lev 27:1–25, 27–29	52
		Num 30:1–16	54
SECOND		Lev 24:15–16	56
Exod 20:4–6	34	**FOURTH**	
Deut 5:8–10	34		
Exod 34:17	35	Exod 20:8–11	58
Lev 19:4	35	Deut 5:12–15	58
Lev 26:1	36	Lev 19:30	60
Exod 20:22–23	36	Lev 26:2	60
Deut 4:12–19, 23–24	36	Exod 23:12	60
Exod 34:14	37	Lev 23:3	60
Deut 11:16–17	37	Exod 31:12–17	60
Deut 8:19–20	37	Exod 34:21	60
Deut 16:22	38	Exod 35:1–3	61
Exod 23:24	38	Lev 19:3	61
Deut 12:4–14, 17–18, 26–27	38		
Deut 14:23–26	40	**FIFTH**	
Exod 20:24–25	40		
Deut 27:5–7	40	Exod 20:12	64
Exod 23:24	41	Deut 5:16	64
Deut 12:1–3	41	Lev 19:3	65
Exod 34:13	41	Exod 21:15, 17	65
Deut 7:5	41	Lev 20:9	65
Num 33:52	42	Deut 21:18–21	65
Deut 16:21	42	Exod 22:28	66
Exod 34:11–12, 15–16	42	Lev 19:32	66
Deut 7:1–4	42	Deut 16:18	67
Exod 23:31–33	43	Deut 20:9	67
Deut 7:16–26	44		
Deut 25:17–19	45		
Deut 23:3–8	46		

Scripture Index A

SIXTH

Exod 20:13	70
Deut 5:17	70
Lev 19:17	70
Lev 19:18	70
Lev 19:14	71
Lev 24:17, 19–22	71
Exod 21:12–14, 18–32	71
Deut 17:6	73
Deut 19:15	73
Deut 22:8	74
Deut 24:7	74
Deut 21:22–23	74
Deut 25:1–3	75
Deut 24:16	75
Deut 20:10–18	75
Deut 23:15–16	76
Deut 22:6–7	77
Exod 23:5	77
Deut 22:4	77
Num 35:9–34	77
Deut 19:1–13	79

SEVENTH

Exod 20:14	82
Deut 5:18	82
Lev 18:20	83
Lev 18:22–30	83
Exod 22:19	89
Lev 20:13, 15–16	89
Lev 19:29	90
Deut 23:17	84
Lev 20:10	90
Deut 22:22–27	90
Lev 19:20–22	91
Exod 21:7–11	84
Exod 22:16–17	92
Deut 24:5	85
Num 5:11–31	85
Deut 22:13–21	92
Deut 24:1–4	93

Lev 18:19	87
Lev 20:18	94
Lev 18:1–4, 6–18	87
Deut 22:30	88
Lev 20:11–12, 14, 17, 19–24	94
Deut 25:11–12	95
Deut 22:12	89
Deut 22:5	89

EIGHTH

Exod 20:15	98
Deut 5:19	98
Lev 19:11, 13	98
Deut 24:14–15	98
Deut 25:4	99
Exod 22:21–24	99
Lev 19:33–34	99
Deut 10:17–19	100
Lev 19:35–36	100
Deut 25:13–16	100
Deut 19:14	101
Exod 22:26–27	101
Deut 24:6, 10–13, 17–18	101
Exod 22:25	102
Lev 25:35–38	102
Deut 23:19–20	103
Deut 22:1–3	104
Exod 23:4	104
Num 5:5–7	104
Exod 23:8	105
Lev 19:15	105
Deut 16:19–20	105
Exod 23:3, 6	106
Exod 22:1–4	106
Exod 22:9	107
Exod 22:5–8, 10–13	107
Exod 22:14–15	108
Lev 24:18, 21	108
Exod 21:33–36	108
Deut 23:24–25	109
Lev 19:9–10	109
Lev 23:22	110

Deut 24:19–22	110
Deut 15:1–11	110
Exod 21:1–6	112
Deut 15:12–18	112
Lev 25:39–55	113
Lev 25:23–34	115
Deut 20:19–20	117
Deut 21:14–17	117
Deut 20:5–8	118
Deut 25:5–10	118

NINTH

Exod 20:16	122
Deut 5:20	122
Exod 23:1–2, 7	123
Lev 19:16–17	123
Deut 19:16–21	123

TENTH

Exod 20:17	126
Deut 5:21	126

SUM OF THE LAW

Deut 10:12–13	128
Deut 6:5	128
Lev 19:18	128

Scripture Index B

Calvin's Decalogical Division in Canonical Order

(Designed for Decalogue scholars, all the Scriptures Calvin uses are presented in canonical order within their respective Decalogical law)

PREFACE

Exod 20:1–2	2
Exod 23:13	8
Exod 23:20–23, 25–31	15
Lev 19:36–37	3
Lev 20:8	3
Lev 22:31–33	3
Lev 27:34	17
Num 15:37–41	8
Deut 1:1–5	17
Deut 4:1–2	3
Deut 4:5–14	4
Deut 4:20	2
Deut 4:32–40	5
Deut 4:44–49	17
Deut 5:1–6	2
Deut 5:32–33	3
Deut 6:1–3, 17–19	14
Deut 6:6–9	8
Deut 6:10–12	10
Deut 6:20–25	7
Deut 7:6–8	6
Deut 8:1–6	12
Deut 8:7–10	13
Deut 8:11–18	14
Deut 9:1–6	10
Deut 10:14–17	6
Deut 10:21–22	11
Deut 11:1–7	11
Deut 11:8–9	12
Deut 11:10–12	13
Deut 11:18–20	8
Deut 13:18	3
Deut 26:16–19	7
Deut 27:1–4, 8	9
Deut 27:9–10	6
Deut 29:1	17
Deut 29:2–9	12
Deut 29:29	16
Deut 30:11–14	16
Deut 31:10–13	9

FIRST

Exod 12:15, 19	28
Exod 20:3	20
Exod 22:18	28
Lev 18:21	23
Lev 19:1–2	21
Lev 19:26, 31	24
Lev 20:1–5	28
Lev 20:6, 27	28
Num 10:1–10	31
Num 15:30–31	28
Deut 5:7	20
Deut 6:4, 13	20
Deut 6:14–15	21
Deut 6:16	20
Deut 10:20	20
Deut 12:29–32	24
Deut 13:1–4	23

Deut 13:5	24	**THIRD**	
Deut 13:6–11	26		
Deut 13:12–17	27	Exod 20:7	50
Deut 17:12–13	25	Exod 23:13	51
Deut 17:14–20	29	Lev 19:12	50
Deut 18:9–14	21	Lev 24:15–16	56
Deut 18:15–18	22	Lev 27:1–25, 27–29	52
Deut 18:19	24	Num 30:1–16	54
Deut 18:21–22	23	Deut 5:11	50
Deut 20:1–4	30	Deut 6:13	51
		Deut 10:20	51
SECOND		Deut 23:21–23	51
Exod 20:4–6	34	**FOURTH**	
Exod 20:22–23	36		
Exod 20:24–25	40	Exod 20:8–11	58
Exod 23:24	38	Exod 23:12	60
Exod 23:24	41	Exod 31:12–17	60
Exod 23:31–33	43	Exod 34:21	60
Exod 34:11–12, 15–16	42	Exod 35:1–3	61
Exod 34:13	41	Lev 19:3	61
Exod 34:14	37	Lev 19:30	60
Exod 34:17	35	Lev 23:3	60
Lev 19:4	35	Lev 26:2	60
Lev 26:1	36	Deut 5:12–15	58
Num 33:52	42		
Deut 4:12–19, 23–24	36	**FIFTH**	
Deut 5:8–10	34		
Deut 7:1–4	42	Exod 20:12	64
Deut 7:5	41	Exod 21:15, 17	65
Deut 7:16–26	44	Exod 22:28	66
Deut 8:19–20	37	Lev 19:3	65
Deut 11:16–17	37	Lev 19:32	66
Deut 12:1–3	41	Lev 20:9	65
Deut 12:4–14, 17–18, 26–27	38	Deut 5:16	64
Deut 14:23–26	40	Deut 16:18	67
Deut 16:21	42	Deut 20:9	67
Deut 16:22	38	Deut 21:18–21	65
Deut 17:2–5, 7	46		
Deut 23:3–8	46	**SIXTH**	
Deut 25:17–19	45		
Deut 27:5–7	40	Exod 20:13	70
		Exod 21:12–14, 18–32	71

Scripture Index B

Exod 23:5	77
Lev 19:14	71
Lev 19:17	70
Lev 19:18	70
Lev 24:17, 19–22	71
Num 35:9–34	77
Deut 5:17	70
Deut 17:6	73
Deut 19:1–13	79
Deut 19:15	73
Deut 20:10–18	75
Deut 21:22–23	74
Deut 22:4	77
Deut 22:6–7	77
Deut 22:8	74
Deut 23:15–16	76
Deut 24:7	74
Deut 24:16	75
Deut 25:1–3	75

SEVENTH

Exod 20:14	82
Exod 21:7–11	84
Exod 22:16–17	92
Exod 22:19	89
Lev 18:1–4, 6–18	87
Lev 18:19	87
Lev 18:20	83
Lev 18:22–30	83
Lev 19:20–22	91
Lev 19:29	90
Lev 20:10	90
Lev 20:11–12, 14, 17, 19–24	94
Lev 20:13, 15–16	89
Lev 20:18	94
Num 5:11–31	85
Deut 5:18	82
Deut 22:5	89
Deut 22:12	89
Deut 22:13–21	92
Deut 22:22–27	90
Deut 22:30	88
Deut 23:17	84

Deut 24:1–4	93
Deut 24:5	85
Deut 25:11–12	95

EIGHTH

Exod 20:15	98
Exod 21:1–6	112
Exod 21:33–36	108
Exod 22:1–4	106
Exod 22:5–8, 10–13	107
Exod 22:9	107
Exod 22:14–15	108
Exod 22:21–24	99
Exod 22:25	102
Exod 22:26–27	101
Exod 23:3, 6	106
Exod 23:4	104
Exod 23:8	105
Lev 19:9–10	109
Lev 19:11, 13	98
Lev 19:15	105
Lev 19:33–34	99
Lev 19:35–36	100
Lev 23:22	110
Lev 24:18, 21	108
Lev 25:23–34	115
Lev 25:35–38	102
Lev 25:39–55	113
Num 5:5–7	104
Deut 5:19	98
Deut 10:17–19	100
Deut 15:1–11	110
Deut 15:12–18	112
Deut 16:19–20	105
Deut 19:14	101
Deut 20:5–8	118
Deut 20:19–20	117
Deut 21:14–17	117
Deut 22:1–3	104
Deut 23:19–20	103
Deut 23:24–25	109
Deut 24:6, 10–13, 17–18	101
Deut 24:14–15	98

Deut 24:19–22	110
Deut 25:4	99
Deut 25:5–10	118
Deut 25:13–16	100

NINTH

Exod 20:16	122
Exod 23:1–2, 7	123
Lev 19:16–17	123
Deut 5:20	122
Deut 19:16–21	123

TENTH

Exod 20:17	126
Deut 5:21	126

SUM OF THE LAW

Lev 19:18	128
Deut 6:5	128
Deut 10:12–13	128

Scripture Index C

Canonical Order

(Designed to locate a verse speedily, all the Scriptures that Calvin uses are presented in canonical order.)

EXODUS	Page / Law
12:15, 19	28 / 1
20:1–2	2 / P
20:3	20 / 1
20:4–6	34 / 2
20:7	50 / 3
20:8–11	58 / 4
20:12	64 / 5
20:13	70 / 6
20:14	82 / 7
20:15	98 / 8
20:16	122 / 9
20:17	126 / 10
20:22–23	36 / 2
20:24–25	40 / 2
21:1–6	112 / 8
21:7–11	84 / 7
21:12–14, 18–32	71 / 6
21:15, 17	65 / 5
21:33–36	108 / 8
22:1–4	106 / 8
22:5–8, 10–13	107 / 8
22:9	107 / 8
22:14–15	108 / 8
22:16–17	92 / 7
22:18	28 / 1
22:19	89 / 7
22:21–24	99 / 8
22:25	102 / 8
22:26–27	101 / 8
22:28	66 / 5
23:1–2, 7	123 / 9
23:3, 6	106 / 8
23:4	104 / 8
23:5	77 / 6
23:8	105 / 8
23:12	60 / 4
23:13	8 / P
23:13	51 / 3
23:20–23, 25–31	15 / P
23:24	38 / 2
23:24	41 / 2
23:31–33	43 / 2
31:12–17	60 / 4
34:11–12, 15–16	42 / 2
34:13	41 / 2
34:14	37 / 2
34:17	35 / 2
34:21	60 / 4
35:1–3	61 / 4

LEVITICUS	
18:1–4, 6–18	87 / 7
18:19	87 / 7
18:20	83 / 7
18:21	23 / 1
18:22–30	83 / 7
19:1–2	21 / 1
19:3	61 / 4
19:3	65 / 5

19:4	35 / 2	5:11–31	85 / 7
19:9–10	109 / 8	10:1–10	31 / 1
19:11, 13	98 / 8	15:30–31	28 / 1
19:12	50 / 3	15:37–41	8 / P
19:14	71 / 6	30:1–16	54 / 3
19:15	105 / 8	33:52	42 / 2
19:16–17	123 / 9	35:9–34	77 / 6
19:17	70 / 6		
19:18	70 / 6		
19:18	128 / S	**DEUTERONOMY**	
19:20–22	91 / 7	1:1–5	17 / P
19:26, 31	24 / 1	4:1–2	3 / P
19:29	90 / 7	4:5–14	4 / P
19:30	60 / 4	4:12–19, 23–24	36 / 2
19:32	66 / 5	4:20	2 / P
19:33–34	99 / 8	4:32–40	5 / P
19:35–36	100 / 8	4:44–49	17 / P
19:36–37	3 / P	5:1–6	2 / P
20:1–5	28 / 1	5:7	20 / 1
20:6, 27	28 / 1	5:8–10	34 / 2
20:8	3 / P	5:11	50 / 3
20:9	65 / 5	5:12–15	58 / 4
20:10	90 / 7	5:16	64 / 5
20:11–12, 14, 17, 19–24	94 / 7	5:17	70 / 6
20:13, 15–16	89 / 7	5:18	82 / 7
20:18	94 / 7	5:19	98 / 8
22:31–33	3 / P	5:20	122 / 9
23:3	60 / 4	5:21	126 / 10
23:22	110 / 8	5:32–33	3 / P
24:15–16	56 / 3	6:1–3, 17–19	14 / P
24:17, 19–22	71 / 6	6:4, 13	20 / 1
24:18, 21	108 / 8	6:5	128 / S
25:23–34	115 / 8	6:6–9	8 / P
25:35–38	102 / 8	6:10–12	10 / P
25:39–55	113 / 8	6:13	51 / 3
26:1	36 / 2	6:14–15	21 / 1
26:2	60 / 4	6:16	20 / 1
27:1–25, 27–29	52 / 3	6:20–25	7 / P
27:34	17 / P	7:1–4	42 / 2
		7:5	41 / 2
NUMBERS		7:6–8	6 / P
		7:16–26	44 / 2
5:5–7	104 / 8	8:1–6	12 / P

8:7–10	13 / P	20:9	67 / 5
8:11–18	14 / P	20:10–18	75 / 6
8:19–20	37 / 2	20:19–20	117 / 8
9:1–6	10 / P	21:14–17	117 / 8
10:12–13	128 / S	21:18–21	65 / 5
10:14–17	6 / P	21:22–23	74 / 6
10:17–19	100 / 8	22:1–3	104 / 8
10:20	20 / 1	22:4	77 / 6
10:20	51 / 3	22:5	89 / 7
10:21–22	11 / P	22:6–7	77 / 6
11:1–7	11 / P	22:8	74 / 6
11:8–9	12 / P	22:12	89 / 7
11:10–12	13 / P	22:13–21	92 / 7
11:16–17	37 / 2	22:22–27	90 / 7
11:18–20	8 / P	22:30	88 / 7
12:1–3	41 / 2	23:3–8	46 / 2
12:4–14, 17–18, 26–27	38 / 2	23:15–16	76 / 6
12:29–32	24 / 1	23:17	84 / 7
13:1–4	23 / 1	23:19–20	103 / 8
13:5	24 / 1	23:21–23	51 / 3
13:6–11	26 / 1	23:24–25	109 / 8
13:12–17	27 / 1	24:1–4	93 / 7
13:18	3 / P	24:5	85 / 7
14:23–26	40 / 2	24:6, 10–13, 17–18	101 / 8
15:1–11	110 / 8	24:7	74 / 6
15:12–18	112 / 8	24:14–15	98 / 8
16:18	67 / 5	24:16	75 / 6
16:19–20	105 / 8	24:19–22	110 / 8
16:21	42 / 2	25:1–3	75 / 6
16:22	38 / 2	25:4	99 / 8
17:2–5, 7	46 / 2	25:5–10	118 / 8
17:6	73 / 6	25:11–12	95 / 7
17:12–13	25 / 1	25:13–16	100 / 8
17:14–20	29 / 1	25:17–19	45 / 2
18:9–14	21 / 1	26:16–19	7 / P
18:15–18	22 / 1	27:1–4, 8	9 / P
18:19	24 / 1	27:5–7	40 / 2
18:21–22	23 / 1	27:9–10	6 / P
19:1–13	79 / 6	29:1	17 / P
19:14	101 / 8	29:2–9	12 / P
19:15	73 / 6	29:29	16 / P
19:16–21	123 / 9	30:11–14	16 / P
20:1–4	30 / 1	31:10–13	9 / P
20:5–8	118 / 8		

www.ingramcontent.com/pod-product-compliance
Lightning Source LLC
Chambersburg PA
CBHW050805160426
43192CB00010B/1644